Last Writings

Nothingness and the Religious Worldview

Nishida Kitarō

Translated with an Introduction by
David A. Dilworth

University of Hawaii Press
Honolulu

Library of Congress Cataloging-in-Publication Data
Nishida, Kitarō, 1870–1945.
   Last writings: nothingness and the religious worldview.
   Essays.
   Translation of: Bashoteki ronri to shūkyōteki
sekaikan, and Watakushi no ronri ni tsuite.
   Includes bibliographies and index.
   1. Religion—Philosophy. 2. Nothing (Philosophy)
I. Nishida, Kitarō, 1879–1945. Watakushi no ronri ni
tsuite. English. 1987. II. Title.
B5244.N553B3713   1987   200′.1   86–30931
ISBN 0-8248-1040-6

Contents

Introduction
Nishida's Critique of the Religious Consciousness

The Gradual Framing of a Logic

Nishida Kitarō, Japan's premier modern philosopher, was born in 1870. He grew to intellectual maturity in the final decades of the Meiji period (1868–1912) and achieved recognition as Japan's leading establishment philosopher during his tenure as professor of philosophy at Kyoto Imperial University in his forties and fifties. After his retirement in 1927, and until his death in 1945, he retained his status as Japan's foremost academic thinker through a constant stream of original publications. His collected works, in nineteen volumes, show a pattern of publication of one major title in every two or three years over an approximately thirty-year period.[1]

Nishida's writings are a prism in which we can see refracted the manifaceted atmosphere of Japanese philosophy in the first half of this century. Nishida was both influenced by, and became a formative influence on, the many waves of intellectual modernization during this period. The special character of his career and works is that they bear witness to a creative assimilation of a complex range of philosophical values stemming from the confluence of Eastern and Western civilizations taking place in his own time. Indeed, together with the penetrating responses to this same interaction of cultures by some of his contemporaries—notably, such literary giants as Natsume Sōseki (1867–1916) and Mori Ōgai (1862–1922)—Nishida's works reflect a level of serious intercivilizational encounter in the twentieth century which perhaps still has no counterpart in our own occidental culture.[2] To the reader of Nishida's writings, it becomes immediately evident that his philosophical discourse extends beyond the confines of regional studies, challenging the insularity of a merely Asian or a merely Western cultural bias, to say nothing of the methodological prejudices of particular academic settings.

Together with Husserl, Whitehead, Heidegger, Wittgenstein, and other prominent philosophers of our times, Nishida's stature looms largest as an original thinker. His chief contribution to twentieth-century thought is in the area of religious philosophy, and in what he called the philosophy of religion. This volume presents translations of the last two essays of Nishida's long career, representing the culmination of his effort to articulate the logic of the religious consciousness. What I am calling Nishida's logic is the discursive form he came to employ to reflect philosophically upon the Buddhist idea of "absolute nothingness."[3] But while the essays translated here exhibit the clarity in articulation which Nishida achieved in the months before he died in 1945, it is important to note that his career-long endeavor to forge viable categories to elucidate the essentially religious ground of experience was characterized by a general reticence in regard to Eastern religious texts. His employment of Eastern, and especially Mahayana Buddhist, concepts always proceeded obliquely, and on a generic level of discourse that permitted encounter, interresonance, and interramification with Western philosophical concepts drawn from such figures as Aristotle, Plotinus and the Christian Neo-Platonists, Spinoza, Leibniz, Kant, Hegel, Husserl, and others. It was only in the last years of his career that Nishida made explicit use of his own religious heritage to illustrate his views.[4]

But again, the reader of these essays will note that Nishida's philosophical strength does not consist in these references to Buddhist sources. It lies rather in his continuing dialogue with the Western philosophers Aristotle, Leibniz, Kant, and Hegel, whose strategic positions in the history of philosophy are emphatically highlighted in Nishida's many writings and incorporated in Nishida's own logic. The various references in these essays to religious thinkers such as Augustine, Luther, Pascal, and Kierkegaard, and to such an existentialist thinker as Dostoievski, are interwoven with references to Buddhist traditions in a manner that well demonstrates the intercivilizational aspect of Nishida's style. Yet the position that Nishida elaborates is one that he came to only by working with what he saw as the contrasting requirements of the Aristotelian logic of "the subject that cannot be predicate" and the Kantian logic of "the predicate that cannot be subject." To resolve this impasse Nishida formulated a new logical paradigm through which he could articulate a doctrine of the "contradictory identity" of the religious self, which he defined as the "true self" that "sees without being a seer and acts while being nothing itself." We shall see that Nishida's articulation of this impasse, and his paradoxical definition of religious individuality, involved a running commentary on the logics of Leibniz and Hegel as well.

According to Nishida's conception of the options in logic after 1927, the Aristotelian "subject that cannot be predicate" entails a paradigmatic form of discourse in respect of objective determination. Nishida refers to this discursive form as the logic of the grammatical subject, or the logic of objects. In this framework of objective intentionality the grammatical subject is a material, or substantive reification—it signifies a *something* that subtends its own predicates. This kind of discourse literally makes a thing *(res)*, a determinate being or essence in a noematic sense. It is determinate precisely by virtue of including its predicates, which characterize it predicamentally—that is, in relation to all other spatial, temporal, and categorial positions in the world.

To some extent Nishida's reading of Aristotle here was mediated by his adherence to Kant, and to Husserl's concept of the noema. What Nishida wants to insist upon is that in this presupposition of objective intentionality every trace of an active knowing subject is absent. Taken to its logical conclusion by Spinoza, the world as noematic determination becomes a single objective essence. Nature (or God) becomes the ultimate substance, and grammatical subject, of every predication. But this would be God or nature one-sidedly conceived of as *natura naturata*.

Nishida insists that a metaphysical analysis must account for this feature of objective reification. But he argues that our experience cannot be rendered intelligible exclusively by it. Here he sides openly with Kant. Every grammatical subject necessarily entails the transcendental forms of the knowing subject which configure it as object. These subjective conditions of objectivity are delineated in Kant's concepts of space and time as pure forms of sensibility, of the a priori categories of the understanding, and of their formal grounding in the unity of apperception. But Kant's transcendental turn, in Nishida's understanding, was taken to another level by Husserl. He agrees with Husserl that the noetic contributions of the knowing subject, which are entirely un-noticed in the natural, objective standpoint, become accessible by reflection upon the constitutive structure of the judicative, or predicative, act. Rather than the grammatical subject including its predicates, reflexive analysis yields the insight that the object only appears in the epistemic field—the transcendental space—of its predicative relations.[5] The fact that the object is "enfolded" within its own a priori conditions entails what Nishida calls "a logic of the predicate."

Nishida worked on this logic of the predicate during the middle years of his career, and his exploration of its inner latticing provides intricate analyses of the forms of subjectivity in the phenomenological style.[6] The key strategy of these analyses is suggested by his phrase "transcending inwardly into the depths of noesis," as Nishida embarked on a veritable *noesis noeseos*—thinking the transcendental conditions of thinking. This effort came finally to reveal a three-tiered structure of cognitive, aesthetic, and volitional acts. These reflexive levels, moreover, are said by Nishida to have a hierarchical pattern of apriority in that the forms of cognitive subjectivity are grounded in the forms of aesthetic and volitional subjectivity. The latter indeed contain the transcendental conditions of the former. But Nishida was still not satisfied with this level of noetic disclosure. His key concept rather became one of self-expression in an *existential* sense. Here Nishida saw himself as going beyond Husserl. In the range of intentional acts a person's propositional knowledge or cognition of what is true is only minimally self-expressive, whereas aesthetic and ethical acts reveal a higher degree of personal content. But even our aesthetic and ethical acts must partake in real human *existence*. To Nishida, real human existence is always concretely *individual*.

But as the self gains in personal awareness, it also becomes increasingly conscious of its own internal contradictions. These contradictions are already met on the cognitive and aesthetic levels of consciousness, but they are even more pronounced in the ethical life wherein the individual must, paradoxically, will a universal moral good. For Nishida, this *aporia* of the ethical self is unresolvable on its own terms, and lures the reflexive self on to discover its own "vanishing point" (Dostoievski) of bottomless contradiction. He seeks to characterize this vanishing point of existential contradiction as the very point of departure for religious awareness.

According to Nishida, truly personal awareness begins from an active intuition of one's own contradictory embodiment of individual historical existence; it develops into a religious insight into the simultaneous revealment of self and world. The *religiosi* of history have attained to realization of God or the Absolute from this standpoint which, according to Nishida, has the form of self-expression through self-negation. He therefore sought to articulate a philosophy that adequately describes the self-transcending act of religious awareness as the ultimate point of ontological reference. The reality of the self and the other (the world, God, the Absolute) is gathered here, or nowhere—in one's own historical-bodily existence.

Now this dynamically tensional structure in which self and world are mutually revealed and ontologically constituted suggested to Nishida yet another logical paradigm, one enveloping both the subject that cannot be predicate and the predicate that cannot be subject. After 1927 he began to refer to this enveloping logic as "the logic of the place of nothingness." He was still working on its articulation in his final essay on the religious consciousness in 1945. In effect, Nishida's paradigm grounds the principle of non-contradiction, which he sees as pertaining to the logic of objects (the subject that cannot be predicate), in a new axiom of "contradictory identity," disclosing, among other things, the codetermining identity of subject and object, and of grammatical subject and predicate. It will be important to note that Nishida's concept of "contradictory identity" is not dialectical (sublational) in a Platonic or Hegelian sense;[7] in his language it does not postulate another level of being or noematic determination. According to Nishida, the "last enveloping place" is to be found neither in the direction of the grammatical subject nor in the direction of the predicate. It is in fact the existential and yet absolute "place" *(basho)* of the irresolvable opposition of these two planes, having a logical form in which each expresses the other in and through its own self-negation.

It was by so framing, and gradually clarifying, this logical form that Nishida opened the way to his articulation of the religious ground of self-consciousness, in which "seeing is acting and acting is seeing" in a perspective of ultimate disclosure. After 1927, Nishida made enormous strides in clarifying the semantically constitutive features of his religious worldview. As we shall see, he thereby came to repossess a Buddhist paradigm of philosophical articulation, although in his own highly original fashion.

Nishida's Challenge to Kant's Second Critique

We have suggested that Nishida's theoretical work over a period of four decades achieved its final form in a philosophy of religion. Let us turn directly to his most comprehensive formulation of this philosophy, "The Logic of the Place of Nothingness and the Religious Worldview" (1945), which has been appreciated as one of Nishida's major works.[8] This essay can also be called the *fons et origo* of the Kyoto School.

In a word, Nishida strove in this long, final essay to write a critique of the religious consciousness. It begins with his career-long insistence that the dimension of authentic religious experience does have a logical form. He always repudiated those species of "mysticism" whose hidden agenda consists in depreciating the possibility of philosophical reflection on the nature of religious experience. Such a depreciation always has its own identifiable methodic strategy, or discursive pattern, notwithstanding its frequent alignment with the "silence of the saints." To Nishida, the philosopher can reflect on the *via negativa* forms of religious expression, including the Zen Buddhist's notorious "method of no method," no less than he can reflect on scientific procedure, the process of aesthetic creativity, or moral behavior.

Nishida's whole philosophical project had thus come to focus upon his concern to articulate that form of life which we commonly call religious. In reading this essay, it is natural to speculate that he must have been a profoundly religious person in the depths of his own soul. Be that as it may, up to two or three days before his death, when he penned his *zeppitsu* or "final words,"[9] he considered his life's work to have consisted in framing a "concrete logic," as opposed to merely describing a religious experience or reenacting a religious position.

Nishida's many theoretical works indicate that he especially appreciated the architectonic nature of Kant's three *Critiques*. During the last twenty-five years of his life he consistently approached the questions of philosophy through the framework of Kant's formulations, which map independent domains of cognitive, moral, and aesthetic subjectivity as part of the architectonic of pure reason itself. In the final analysis, however, Kant gives only a subordinate role to the religious consciousness and this always suggested to Nishida that a space remained open for another critique that would delineate the autonomous domain of the existential, and religious, consciousness.

"The Logic of the Place of Nothingness and the Religious Worldview" can be read as Nishida's challenge to Kant, and especially to the conclusions of the *Critique of Practical Reason*. Nishida in fact begins his essay with several allusions to Kant's second *Critique*. Referring to its principle of pure (practical) reason as the standpoint of "mere reason" *(blosse Vernunft)*, Nishida proceeds forthwith to suggest that religious subjectivity cannot be adequately articulated from that standpoint. There is a weakness, according to Nishida, in Kant's manner of regarding the immortality of the soul and the existence of God as "mere postulates" of the moral will. By rethinking Kant's position, Nishida intends to bring these central questions of *religio* to the forefront of his own philosophy, with the aim of achieving a reconstruction of Kant's conceptual priorities in regard to the moral and religious domains of subjectivity.

Since this contrapuntal relation to Kant's second *Critique* is maintained as a dominant motif in the "Religious Worldview" essay, let us briefly examine Kant's position before proceeding to an in-depth discussion of Nishida's text. Kant's second *Critique* does in fact provide a formal justification of the concepts of the immortality of the soul and the existence of God under the rubric of their being postulates of the principle of pure practical reason, or of the pure moral will. Religion to Kant is a matter of rational

faith—that is, of faith in the domain of the pure moral intention
and its consequences. He heaps scorn upon the concept of an
autonomous "holy will"—that is, a putative form of subjectivity
that could be free of the obligating imperative of the moral law
disclosed in the legislative act of the moral will itself. It is almost
as if Kant had in mind the variety of Ch'an (Zen) Buddhist and
other existentialist religious positions with which Nishida sometimes aligns his own thought. To be sure, Kant did not have direct
knowledge of the Mahayana Buddhism of which Ch'an is a notable exponent in its religious practice and teaching. Nishida, however, was steeped in both Kant and the Mahayana traditions, and
could accordingly adjudicate the issues at hand.

For his part Kant regards the alternative to his view—the
concept of a "holiness of will"—as a species of "dialectical illusion." He characterizes this alternative position as "theosophis-
tic" and associates it in several contexts with religious and moral
"fanaticism." The dialectical illusion exhibited in this view
stems from a confusion, or a deliberate collapsing, of the phenomenal and noumenal domains of causality into a single, existential realm. It had been the arduous task of the *Critique of Pure
Reason* to demonstrate the illegitimacy of such a conflation of
appearance and reality, or of the domains of phenomenal and
noumenal causality, respectively.

The Critique of Practical Reason is Kant's "metaphysics of
morals." In the concluding paragraph of the work he speaks of the
prospect which it opens up for a "science" of the moral life that
will be "critically sought and methodically directed."[10] In the
present context, the pertinent feature of this last expression is
that it reveals, in encapsulated version, the hermeneutical profile
of Kant's whole text. If the autonomous moral will is the second
Critique's ultimate ontological focus, its methodic articulation
as a synoptic analysis of the a priori structure of the moral will is
organized in reference to the reflexive *telos* of pure practical reason itself. Kant's synoptic method of articulation in the service of
the self-legislating principle of pure reason—that is what "critique" means—and his ontological focus (the noumenal domain
of the co-determining moral will and moral law) are thus the formal and material causes, respectively, of his second *Critique*.

Kant's *Critique* has its place in the broader architectonic framework of the three *Critiques* and the various subsidiary writings of his critical philosophy. Through this theoretical labor, Kant sought to lay the foundation of a critical metaphysics, or "metaphysics as science," which could display "the inventory of all our possessions of pure reason, systematically arranged."[11] His metaphysics of morals constitutes one facet of this broader critical project. Pure reason's reflexive principle of legislating its own essential forms in a complete set functions variably as the integrating semantic assumption in these writings; it guides the speculative and practical employments of pure reason to transparent self-completion and satisfaction in the process of its own self-reflection on its own essential parts, or domains.

The "old metaphysics," with its hyperbolical claims of theoretical knowledge as to transphenomenal and unconditioned realities (the concepts of God, freedom, and immortality in their illegitimate transcendent use), Kant therefore set out to deny as uncritically dogmatic. He envisioned his new "metaphysics as science" to be entirely possible under the guidance of the principle of pure reason—that is, of active reason thinking itself in respect of its own preconditions—and of his synoptic method of articulation of these preconditions. Here again Kant was following his mentor, Aristotle, whose own thought exhibits a reflexive principle ("thought thinking itself," *noesis noeseos*) in conjunction with a problematic method in a scientific, or disciplinary, perspective. Aristotle had distinguished the theoretical, practical, and productive functions of active reason in his own architectonic science of the sciences. Kant's three *Critiques* are in effect a translation of Aristotle's project into his own transcendental mapping of our rational faculties.

Kant's architectonic "metaphysics as science" mapped two fundamentally different kinds of causality, the physical and the moral, corresponding to the subject matters of his first two *Critiques*. His "metaphysics of nature," critically grounded and methodically framed in terms of the a priori forms of sensibility and of the understanding, exhibits the "complete physiological table" of all the transcendental forms of *Sein*—of what is, or can appear, in the judicative domain of physical causation. His "metaphysics of morals" displays the formal conditions of the ethical *Sollen*, or what ought to be, in the domain of moral causation. Neither *Critique* envisions the justification of the transcendent concepts of God, freedom, and immortality in terms of a cognitive access to unconditioned realities, or what Kant calls things-in-themselves. These latter significations remain for Kant merely immanent, subjective ideals of pure reason; but they lead to dialectical illusions when given a transcendent, objective reference.

"Critique" therefore meant for Kant the self-reflection of pure reason on its own forms and possibilities. Negatively, it functions to curb the dogmatic and fanatical claim of speculative or practical reason in their dialectical use; positively, it determines the structures, scope, and proper employment of valid, objective concepts.[12] In his first *Critique* Kant is an Aristotelian, albeit a transcendental one, in seeking to delineate the essential outlines of the universal, a priori structures exhibited and presupposed in scientific practice in respect of the domain of phenomenal, or natural, causation. In his second *Critique*, however, he is a Platonist in regard to the supersensible "intelligible world" of the moral subject and the moral law.[13] Thus in the latter *Critique* Kant refers to the concepts of "the kingdom of God" and "the glory of God" in implicit allusion to Leibniz, whose ontological language of a Platonic world of spirit-monads forms the background to Kant's own noumenal signification of the realm of pure moral will.[14] We shall see that Nishida understood Kant's relation to Leibniz in these same terms.

In the second *Critique* there are numerous expressions of the conjunction of Kant's self-legislating rational principle with his synoptic method, which correspond to the "critically sought and methodically directed" operators of his science of morals. He formulates this conjunction when he writes:

> When it is a question of determining the origin, contents, and limits of a particular faculty of the human mind, the nature of human knowledge makes it impossible to do otherwise than begin with an exact and (as far as is allowed by the knowledge we have already gained) complete delineation of its parts. But still another thing must be attended to which *is of a more philosophical and architectonic character.* It is to grasp correctly the idea of the whole, and then to see all those parts in their reciprocal interrelations, in the light of their derivation from the concept of the whole, and as

united in a pure rational faculty. This examination and the attainment of such a view are obtainable only through a most intimate acquaintance with the system. Those who are loath to engage in the first of these inquiries and who do not consider acquiring this acquaintance worth the trouble will not reach the second stage, the *synoptic view*, which is a synthetic return to that which was previously given only analytically. It is not be be wondered at if they find inconsistencies everywhere, though the gaps which they presume to find are not in the system itself but in their own incoherent train of thought.[15]

Kant proceeds to formulate, in a scientifically deductive manner, the "fundamental moral law" and its correlative theory of moral freedom, under the guidance of the same operators of his text—the principle of a pure, self-legislating rational faculty and its synoptic method.

As is well known, Kant argues that the categorical moral imperative is an unconditioned, or absolute, practical rule which extends to all rational beings, not excepting God as a supreme intelligence. Pure reason, legislative and practical in and for itself, here directly signifies a "pure will" that is determined by its own moral *Sollen*, the form of the moral law itself. The fundamental moral law is declared by pure reason to be a law for all rational beings precisely insofar as they have a pure will, a faculty of self-determination through the concept of a rule of conduct, and accordingly insofar as they are competent to so determine their ethical behavior in the form of the *Sollen*.

It is in this pivotal context of the second *Critique*'s deduction of the fundamental law of pure practical reason that Kant attacks the concept of a "holy will."

> For though we can suppose that men as rational beings have a pure will, since they are affected by wants and sensuous motives we cannot suppose them to have a holy will, a will incapable of any maxims which conflict with the moral law.[16]

Such a concept of holiness would elevate freedom above obligation and duty. But this kind of "holiness of will," Kant argues, only has the character of a practical ideal; it is incapable of perfect existential realization. He contrasts this with the "constancy of virtue," which is exhibited in our making continuous moral progress in this life (and, indeed, in all eternity). The life of virtue, being a naturally acquired capacity, "can never be perfect, because assurance in such a case never becomes apodictic certainty, and as a mere opinion it is very dangerous."[17]

Kant returns to this point in several places in his second *Critique*. He interprets the teaching of the Gospel, "Love God above all and thy neighbor as thyself," as a *moral command* not groundable in the inclinations of love that is "pathological"—his term for a love that is determined in the domain of phenomenal, or natural, causation. The Gospel command, the "law of all laws," presents the moral disposition in its complete perfection. And yet it remains only "an ideal of holiness . . . unattainable by any creature,"[18] an archetype which we should strive to approach and to imitate in an uninterrupted moral progress. Virtue would cease to be moral in the case of a merely "pathological" love for the Gospel injunction. Thus once more, in the spirit of preventing both religious and moral fanaticism, Kant repudiates the validity of the concept of "a spontaneous inclination" to virtue which is free of the constraining feature of moral duty. Rather, the condition of freedom which a person can always achieve is again that of virtue, that is, "moral disposition in conflict, and not holiness in the supposed possession of perfect purity of the intentions of the will."[19]

Kant's rejection of the concept of a perfect, spontaneous moral realization is a pervasive theme in his text; it is present whenever he argues against the possibility of a moral reason having the character of something pathologically conditioned by a sensual principle of happiness. Thus he pours invective on "Mohammed's paradise or the fusion with the deity of the sophists and mystics, according to the tastes of each." It would be better to have no reason at all, Kant opines, than "to surrender it in such a manner to all sorts of dreams."[20] His own argument for the immortality of the soul and the existence of God as practical postulates of the infinitely progressing moral will is the reverse side of this critical coin. These questions of *religio* as postulates of our rational faith logically depend upon the apodictic deduction of the moral law from the principle of pure practical reason itself.

Kant's positive thesis concerning "the moral destiny of our nature" is thus articulated in opposition to what he calls "fanatical theosophical dreams," that is, "a hoped-for complete attainment of holiness of will" in this life.[21] He states his positive justification of our moral destiny in the framework of Book Two, "The Dialectic of Pure Reason in General." As noted above, by *dialec tic*, in both its speculative and practical employment, Kant refers to pure reason's natural propensity to demand an absolute totality of conditions for a given conditioned thing. And yet the whole thrust of his *Critique of Pure Reason* was to show how this is essentially impossible for human experience. For human experience is ineluctably of appearances, or phenomena, in an unending chain of relative conditions in which the unconditioned can in principle never appear. It follows "that an unavoidable illusion arises from the application of the rational idea of the totality of conditions (and thus of the unconditioned) to appearances as if they were things-in-themselves."[22] Kant grounds his postulates of the immortality of the soul and the existence of God in the principle of pure practical reason precisely in order to avoid this dialectical illusion of the pure speculative reason. In the course of doing so, the thing-in-itself takes its primary ontological form as the acting moral person, a kind of Leibnizian spirit-monad acting in a transphenomenal, noumenal realm.

In sum, Kant repudiates the possibility of collapsing the appearance-reality distinction into either a moral or a religious existentialism. Such a fusion with the deity of the sophists and the mystics in this life represents a form of the dialectical illusion of pure reason in its practical employment. His "paradoxical demand to regard one's self, as subject to freedom, as a noumenon, and yet from the point of view of nature to think of one's self as a phenomenon in one's own empirical consciousness"[23] is a concise summary of the ontological significations of his first two *Critiques*, each of which is ordered by the principle of self-reflection and logically articulated through a synoptic method. (Nishida, by contrast, will unite the two significations through his logic of contradictory identity in the service of a principle of religious self-awareness.) Kant recapitulates this dual signification in the beautiful concluding passage of the *Critique of Practical Reason*:

. . . the starry heavens above me and the moral law within me. I do not merely conjecture them and seek them as though obscured in

darkness or in the transcendent region beyond my horizon; I see
them before me, and I associate them directly with the consciousness of my own existence.[24]

Kant clearly sees a "paradox" of human existence. He sees the
contradictory identity, in Nishida's language, of *natural causation*
—represented by the indefinite chain of phenomenal causes
which implicates one's body and emotions in the cosmic forces
that move the stars—and my discovery of myself as a free *moral
agent*, the absolutely first in the series of my own determinations. Nevertheless, Kant deals with this paradox in a manner
which remains true to the principle, method, and the ultimately
noumenal ontological focus of his critical philosophy.

Nishida, for his part, expressed his admiration of Kant's
"starry heavens above me and the moral law within me" in virtu-
ally all of his major works. The corpus of his writings, as I have
indicated above, exhibits a deep appreciation of Kant's architectonic of pure reason, but it also reveals his gradual assimilation of
the German philosopher's major categories into his own original,
and highly sophisticated, thought structure. It is almost possible
to say that Nishida's career culminated in his re-articulation of
Kant's "paradoxical demand" in the broader framework of his
own project to develop a "concrete logic" that would incorporate
Kant's logic of the field of transcendental predicates. This philosophical reflection that extended over twenty-five years achieved
its final focus in "The Logic of the Place of Nothingness and the
Religious Worldview," the pervasive logic of which is indeed "paradoxical" in the precise sense we shall spell out below. Taking up
the challenge of Kant's conclusions once again, Nishida's final
essay responds as an articulation of the missing "fourth Critique"
on the existential religious consciousness which we can now see
Kant himself would have regarded as impossible in principle.

Nishida's Existential Matrix Ontology

Turning now to the details of Nishida's reconstruction of the
priorities of Kant's second *Critique*, we will observe that Nishida
succeeds, within the framework of his own logic, in reversing
Kant's definition of the relation between religious and moral self-

consciousness. He accomplishes this by privileging a sense of existential realization as locative of the very creative dynamism of God or the Absolute. This entailed for Nishida a complete assimilation of the sense-constituting factors of Kant's text into his own.[25]

The first section of "The Logic of the Place of Nothingness and the Religious Worldview" will appear to be particularly technical to readers approaching Nishida for the first time, at least in contrast to the ensuing four sections which formulate Nishida's religious philosophy in more familiar language drawn from the spiritual traditions of East and West. In fact, the opening section is nothing less than a condensed version of Nishida's "logic of nothingness" itself, incorporating many of the *Philosophical Essays* Nishida had written between 1935 and 1945. Such substantial essays in their own right as "Life," "The Physical World," and "The Standpoint of Active Intuition" are transistorized, as it were, and integrated into the essay's opening statement.

Another aspect of the same difficulty is that Nishida proceeds forthwith to exhibit his logical operator, which, in reference to the matrices of the physical, biological, and historical-existential (or human) "worlds," is always articulated by counterposing the positions of Aristotle and Kant. Aristotle's logic of the grammatical subject accounts for the noematic determination of enduring objects, essences, or substances; Kant's logic of the field of transcendental predicates accounts for the constituting features of subjectivity. Nishida's own logical operator appears in various forms, but most directly in the Japanese term *basho*—literally, "place," and by extension "field" (as in the concept of "physical field"), "matrix" or "medium," and even "world" (although Nishida can also employ the common term *sekai* for the last of these). *Basho* signifies both the structural matrix in which the logical operation of the contradictory identity of grammatical subject and transcendental predicate obtains, and a governing principle of the world's existential identity, immediacy, and simultaneity—what Nishida calls "the absolute present." But Nishida also signifies that the absolute present of our lives is existentially eschatological, or religious, in its ground. It is the place *(basho)* of our realization of the absolute, and of the absolute's own self-realization, or self-determination.

Every religious person, and especially the paradigmatic lives and utterances of the world's *religiosi*, bears witness to this point.

In the opening section of his essay Nishida rings various changes on what we can describe as a multileveled matrix analysis. The term *basho*, "place" or "matrix," generates semantic changes corresponding to its positioning in the overall latticing of a priori frameworks, each with its distinct presuppositions. In this sense there are for Nishida distinct *basho;* but then these distinctions have their places in the final enveloping *basho*, the *mu no basho*, or "place of nothingness." That final *basho* of nothingness is paradoxically the fullness of the existential present. It is the only concrete *basho*.

Typically, Nishida begins with the physical world, which is to him the most abstract matrix of interacting forces. He builds up from this level to the biological, and finally to the human (historical-existential) worlds to illustrate progressively more concrete versions of his master-concept of the "absolute present" as a self-transforming matrix of the many and the one. Each of these "worlds" presupposes and exhibits the contradictory identity of objectivity and subjectivity, indicating the respective places of object logic and transcendental logic in a transpositional structure that progressively unfolds its own "concrete logic" and its most adequate exemplification in the historical-existential world. The consummate form of this final "place" of self-awareness, Nishida will argue, is the intimately personal dimension of the autonomous religious self.

The physical world, then, is the *object* world par excellence (although its very *objectivity* still covertly presupposes the constituting forms of transcendental *subjectivity*). It is the Democritean world, purely *material* in ontological signification—atoms acting and reacting in the void, the world of extended substances or masses with purely quantitative properties. Nishida comments at this point that properly speaking there is no real interactivity at this level of merely spatial extensiveness. The concept of the *dynamic* reciprocity of the atoms in the physical system is already bootlegged, as it were, from the biological and historical-existential matrices. A truly active being would not be something merely moved by another, something merely acted upon; it would equally move the other through itself and be active from itself. Thus Nishida follows Aristotle, perhaps by way of Leibniz, in arguing that we cannot properly conceive of *active, energetic* beings in the Democritean world if it is reduced to spatial extensiveness, a world of merely quantitative properties.[26] This argument becomes the point of departure for Nishida's turn toward a more adequate version of the transformational ontology he is formulating. Nishida's argument, in a nutshell, is as follows. The biological world is continuous, on one end, with the physical world and, on the other end, with the human-historical world. In other respects it is its own matrix *(basho)* of self-transformation. Paraphrasing Leibniz, Nishida argues that the concept of a truly active living being entails the predicates of order and continuation. This further entails a concept of irreversible time. It is of the essence of a biological system to reproduce itself. Each pulsation of life is a unique vector of the biological system. The biological world endures in and through its own transformations. It is dynamically formative, organic, and teleological—properties absent at that abstract level we have identified as the physical world.

The biological world, as the matrix of the contradictory identity of one and many, of universal and particular, of species and individual, thus exhibits the structural characteristics of a "world." At the same time it has the form of a dynamic vector, an irreversible movement "from the formed to the forming." The first of these, the transpositional language of one-in-many and many-in-one, exemplifies Nishida's logical operator; the second, his text's integrating presupposition of autonomous world-expression.

It will be seen, then, that to Nishida a transformational ontology is already superimposed upon the physical world to provide it with its basic concept of active force. What is here referred to as superimposition is another name for the transcendental framework always presupposed in the background of the physical world. Leibniz's conception of the coequation of efficient and final causes involves, in Nishida's understanding, this contradictory identity of Aristotelian and Kantian logics. It is this logical coequation which is exhibited, albeit in a still primitive form, in the biological world. The biological world is decidedly not just an *object* world: the interactivity of objective and *subjective* dimensions of life is disclosed in the concept of self-expressive *organisms* and the self-expressive *organic world*. It is this logical matrix of mutual expression that accounts for the general eidos of organisms, their origin and mutation as species through organismic adaptation to environment, and their relations to one another in reproductive, predator-prey, and other such mutualistic interactions.[27]

With this reflexive capacity for expression, the biological world exhibits the biconditional structure of mutual negation and affirmation which Nishida will finally ground in the human world of self-consciousness. Its self-organizing, self-transforming character becomes an analogue of the creative "act" in the existential mode of human awareness. Nishida's multidimensional ontology thus finds adequate conceptualization only at the level of human interactivity and interexpression. Nishida thematizes the I-Thou relation of intersubjectivity, expressed in many of his earlier writings, to this effect.[28] In contrast to Aristotle and Kant, the ontological focus of Nishida's text is existential precisely in its pervasive emphasis on the uniquely expressive "act" which reflects the other. Each act of consciousness actively reflects the world as a unique perspective of the world. But it is simultaneously reflected in the other, and by the world. Nishida builds his ontology on that point.

Nishida's world of human-historical existence is precisely the fluent world of consciousness described negatively in Plato's *Theaetetus*, and positively in William James' *Essays in Radical Empiricism*. Knowledge, he insists, can never transcend its experiential basis. In the sciences, worlds of abstract concepts, which appear to transcend the immediacy of active intuition, come to be engendered; but science cannot get away from its own basis in the individual experience of the historical world. In the final analysis, the Nishidan world creates its own space-time character by taking each monadic "act of consciousness" as a unique position in the calculus of its own transformations. The theoretical and practical sciences of Aristotle and Kant are declared to be "merely abstract" in relation to these creative moments of lived experience.

Concurrently with this shift to an existential mode of ontological signification, Nishida's text espouses and exhibits the principle of absolute simultaneity or identity *(dōitsu)* as the final integrating factor of these matrical analyses. If in Aristotle and Kant—and again, in authors on whom Nishida repeatedly comments such as Descartes, Spinoza, Hegel, and Husserl—the final organizing principle is a rationally reflexive one, then the contrasting semantic *telos* of Nishida's philosophy is suggested by his ubiquitous use of the language of spontaneous world-realization. His motive idea, namely religious awareness in a dimension of absolute freedom, presupposes this absolute identity of the existential self and the world that transcends yet includes the rational consciousness. In other terms, the reflexive principle of the self-completion of reason is to Nishida not archic, or foundational. What is primal, or primordial, is rather the world's irrational, and pre-rational, concrete immediacy. This is Nishida's principle of the self-determination of the dynamically concrete world of the "absolute present." Nishida does not denigrate our rational functions, but sees even the most abstract deliverances of the physical and mathematical sciences as having their concrete ground in what he calls active intuition. The world's immediate, dynamic character is the final ground of the meaning of "active" in his notion of active intuition, which always entails the mutual revealment of self and world.

The same principle subtends his entire logic of world-poesis in which the existential "act" is seen as a transformative world-vector. In these terms it should be apparent that Nishida is well prepared to reconstruct the foundational assumptions of Kant. His textual strategy, I have said, calls for a shift in basic semantic —or sense-constituting—priorities. Nishida's text presents a version of "the self-presencing of the absolute" as a fundamentally religious perspective on the concrete stream of immediately lived experience. His ontological focus—what he often calls "the historical-formative act"—is his text's material cause, so to speak, while its paradoxical articulation through the logic of "contradictory identity," by means of which this existential sense of reality is grounded in a religiously consummatory principle of nondual co-origination, is the formal cause of Nishida's text.

These semantic priorities are all exhibited when he writes that the existential self ("act") is simultaneously an expressed and expressive monad of the world. Each "act" is the Archimedean point of the co-origination of space and time. The historical world is thus to be rendered as self-determining through its own self-expression, which takes the form of ,the "absolute present" configuring itself in the "act of consciousness." The essentially self-conscious "act" thus reflects the world itself as a unique coincidence of every transcendent and immanent plane of historical co-origination. It is radically transformative as a monadic vector of the world's self-expression.

Nishida's fundamental point is that this formulation of the "historical-formative act" as the existential determination of the "absolute present" both incorporates and yet falls outside the conceptual nets of either Aristotle's logic of the grammatical subject or Kant's logic of the transcendental predicate. He rings various changes on the possibilities of discourse in the respective frameworks of Aristotle and Kant, only to show how they are to be returned to the more concretely lived matrix of the "historical space of the absolute present." In this vein he writes: "From my standpoint, the *Ding-an-sich* is nothing other than the transforming matrix in which the self finds itself—the matrix of the self-forming historical world that is immediately expressed in the self."

We shall see further implications of this position as we turn to a consideration of Nishida's logic of the religious consciousness. It is a position in which the "absolute present" and the "nothingness" of the Buddhist traditions are equivalent concepts, although Nishida's philosophical articulation of that equivalence is his own.

Nishida's Logic of the Religious Consciousness

Nishida's essay proceeds to develop his critique of the religious consciousness through a variety of ramifications. Vivid and moving concepts of existential mortality, of the face to face encounter of absolute and relative, of God/Buddha's love and compassion, of the sacred as the transvaluation of all values, and of religious individuality are framed in the paradoxical terms of his "logic of nothingness." Profoundly religious in perspective, Nishida's text endeavors to provide the philosophical articulation of the "faith" and "enlightenment" experiences central to several major religious traditions.

The theme of existential mortality is Nishida's entering wedge over against Kant's second *Critique* and its subordination of the religious consciousness. We have seen that to Nishida the physical and biological worlds become intelligible through the forms of predication based on the primacy of the Aristotelian grammatical subject with its noematic logic of substance and attributes. On the other hand, the world of consciousness in its various theoretical and practical aspects is to be understood as the determinations of the Kantian realm of transcendental predicates. Nishida now argues that neither paradigm, Aristotelian or Kantian, can account for the historical self as an individual self-conscious being that knows of its own mortality. It is only when the self becomes aware of its own existential contradiction—of the fact that it is a unique living being that must die—that the religious problem arises.

Now biological beings, Nishida contends, cannot properly be said to be aware in this way at all. Existential awareness pertains to one's own noetic life. I can never be aware of my own mortality by objectifying myself as a biological being (i.e., as grammatical subject, or object of judgment). My noematic life is merely the life of the flesh and of the species in general. On the other hand, when I am conscious of my self as an active rational being, and act morally in Kant's noumenal or intelligible realm, I by Kant's definition transcend the biological and the historical realms. As a moral being I exist and act in reference to the Idea of the Good which transcends both my biological and historical-existential life.[29] Hence death does not pertain to myself in my universal, rational consciousness either. We shall see that Nishida's text dovetails with Kierkegaard's on this point. The Kantian moral self of pure practical reason, Nishida concludes, "exists in itself but does not die in itself," and accordingly "for [pure] reason to be conscious of its own death has no meaning." From the standpoint of morality, which determines for itself the universal moral law, my self-contradictory *existence* does not even become problematic. It becomes problematic only in that dimension of self-awareness in which *I know of my own death*. Only therein do I embody simultaneously *my life and my death*.

Several volumes of Nishida's *Philosophical Essays* (1935–45) form the background of the point he is making here. In the present essay Nishida cites Pascal's metaphor of the human being as a "thinking reed" *(roseau pensant)*. Though the whole universe should crush a man, because he *knows* that he dies, he has a greater dignity than that which crushes him. This paradoxical form of self-awareness has nothing to do with the universal moral determination of the noumenal self of pure practical reason. It rather points to the autonomous domain of the religious form of self-awareness. (We can note in passing that Nishida is able to illustrate his logic of contradictory identity from either Asian or Western philosophical sources.)

Nishida's "fourth Critique" proceeds to bring many aspects of religious consciousness into a consistent focus. His sense of existential paradox resonates with that of both Pascal and Kierkegaard. For example, a Kierkegaardian as well as Pascalian theme of the relation between the finite, relative self and the absolute being of God surfaces in the consideration of the self's awareness of its own mortality. But to Nishida, "by facing the absolute" the self becomes all the more aware of its own eternal death and nothingness. Rather than the religious paradox generating the Kierkegaardian movement into infinity—in a remembrance of its own eternal consciousness—Nishida holds that the existential self, in facing the absolute, must die to all eternity. This is not some future-oriented "being toward death," however. It means to die *now*, in the existential present of the "absolute now." To be religious means to transcend inwardly into one's own "vanishing point" (Dostoievski) that is simultaneously the absolute's bottomless self-contradiction in the form of the "eternal now" (Dōgen). To Nishida, this reinterpreted existential fact is the primordial one for the religious consciousness, and it is indeed the true point of departure for the religious question. As we probe our own labyrinthine depths we must encounter the minotaur—the absolute—and we must die. The illusion of self-existence is devoured in that one decisive encounter with absolute life or death.

Such must have the seventy-five-year-old philosopher's own thoughts as he fathomed the meaning of his own imminent death. (He died two months later.) True to his philosophical resolve, however, Nishida probed these reflections to the point of their paradoxical inversion—to their resurrection in a religious insight into the absolute indifference of existential life and death and of eternal life and death. If the existential lives in the absolute, the absolute lives in the existential; and conversely, if the existential dies in the absolute, the absolute dies in the existential. But again, as the existential dies in the absolute, the absolute lives in the existential; and conversely, as the absolute dies in the existential, the existential lives in the absolute.

Nishida maintains that the logic of the grammatical subject proves entirely inadequate at this point. A *relative being* cannot even be said to oppose an *absolute being*. To oppose an absolute being it must die, and pass into nothingness. But conversely, an absolute *being* that merely opposed a relative *being* would not be a true absolute, either. It would likewise fall prey to the noematic logic of determinate things and therefore become relative too.

Nishida thus argues that the absolute must be conceived of in such a way that it does not "merely transcend or destroy the relative." We have seen that, among other things, his text's existential focus functions to collapse the traditional appearance and reality distinction; and it accomplishes this precisely through its logic of contradictory identity. The concept of God cannot then be advanced to de-realize the world; but the converse of this is equally true—the "God is dead" motif of modern atheism notwithstanding. (Nishida says that we are not Nietzschean Overmen, but "servants of the Lord.") Furthermore, Nishida's principle of absolute simultaneity and identity governs this entire paradoxical articulation of the relation between the absolute and the relative. Therefore, he argues, each must express the other through its own self-negation. The absolute, which does not exist *on one side* of this transpositional logical form, is necessarily to be conceived of in a nondualistic fashion in respect of the "act of consciousness" itself. Thus the existential "act" is the very stand-in, the "place" of the absolute.

The semantic priorities and strategies of Nishida's text are also suggested by his characterization of this nondualistic "place of nothingness" as a "formless form." One merit of his citing this ancient phrase—versions of which can be traced in Buddhist, Taoist, and Neo-Shinto texts—is that it directly exhibits the paradoxical structure of the very logical operator which his text puts into play. Once this is clearly seen it becomes possible to identify other semantic resonances in such pivotal phrases as "absolute

nothingness" and "place of nothingness." In respect of his existential ontology of world-realization, "nothingness" can support
the signification of "no-thing-ness," where "thing" *(res)* is presupposed to signify a reification in the noematic mode—an
eidetic sense or meaning, an enduring object, or substance, and
the like. "Nothingness" also associates with Nishida's principle
of contradictory identity in that his concept of the absolute
entails the character of a self-determining ground in its own
concrete immediacy. It is a nondiscriminatory, or an indifferent,
immediacy such that every "act" becomes the "expedient
means" *(upaya)*, as the very "dharma-position," of the absolute's
own existential self-realization.

Nishida captures further resonances of this theme when he
cites the ancient Buddhist expression: "Having No Place wherein
it abides, this Mind arises." Nishida's "place of nothingness" is
suggested by "Having No Place wherein it abides," and this functions logically as the transpositional form of negation (non-
attachment). What is ontologically real, namely "this Mind" of
existential religious realization, is logically ordered by the form
of negation in respect of the principle of simultaneous world-realization, which is suggested by "arises." "Not abiding" and "aris-
ing" constitute, respectively, the formal and the final causes in
this expression, while "this mind" corresponds to its material
cause. Since "this Mind" is existential religious realization, or
"*bodhi*-mind" in the Buddhist framework, it signifies the co-real-
ization of one's own religious mind and the Buddha-mind, the co-
origination and nonduality of samsara and nirvana, and other
such concepts that exhibit the same logical form.

Nishida's text sometimes remains elusive because he does
not make these semantic distinctions. Certain rhetorically effective phrases, which conjoin the functions of grounding principle,
discursive method, and ontological focus, can be found in any
philosopher's text. Nishida employs many such phrases in the
course of expressing his ideas, and in considering the form of his
text it seems particularly important semantically to unpack these
phrases which may simultaneously commingle religious, philosophical, cultural, and even ideological connotations. At the least
the reader of his text must be prepared to deal with such highly
charged, and fissionable, materials as Nishida's definition of the

"absolute" as "absolute nothingness" or "absolute negation," and his even more perplexing allusions to an "Asian nothingness" (tōyōteki mu) or "Asian logic" (tōyōteki ronri).[30]

The "absolute," Nishida tells us, is truly absolute by "being opposed to nothing." This formulation, reminiscent of a similar expression in the text of Nicolas of Cusa which Nishida admired,[31] has to be read in conjunction with other recurrent formulations such as "the absolute cannot be a One." The first phrase encapsulates Nishida's point that there can be nothing standing over against the absolute to relativize it. The second signifies that the absolute cannot be or become a One, one-sidedly or substantively. These considerations point to the same semantic operator—contradictory identity—that we have discussed above. Nishida is again saying that the "objective logics" of non-contradiction and dialectical synthesis are inapplicable to the articulation of the true absolute. Even this statement is redundant: it can be reduced to the more precise one that neither is the adequate logic of religious awareness. For religious awareness is a special kind of self-awareness, with its own "subjective logic."

Nishida openly affirms that the absolute is "self-contradictory." It "absolutely negates itself in itself." He thus writes, for example, ". . . because there is Buddha, there are sentient beings; and because there are sentient beings, there is Buddha." It should be noted that the co-implication of the polar opposites, Buddha and sentient beings, is framed in the transpositional form. It would miss the mark entirely to designate the Buddha as the absolute, or as "absolute negation" or "absolute nothingness," in the nominative sense. Nishida's whole text stands against this usage. Buddha and sentient beings, the polar opposites of religious signification, are rather related in and through the logical matrix designated by such rhetorical devices.

The principle which controls this discursive form is that of the self-determining activity ("act") of the absolute. Or again, it is the principle of a deep and dark Urgrund—an Ungrund, if you will, of the absolute simultaneity and identity of the absolute and the relative. Nishida was well aware that this principle of his text was isomorphic with that of major religious texts of both the East and the West. It is a version, for example, of the Buddhist principle of *sunyata*, and again of the One of Plotinus, Meister Eckhart, Boehme, and Cusanus.

But among other things this consideration exposes a certain rhetorical, and polemical, nuance that is built into his concepts of "nothingness" and "Asian nothingness," especially when he formulated them as counterparts to "being" and "Western being." In employing the nominative "nothingness" to designate his absolute, Nishida can be charged with having chosen one-sidedly between conceptual opposites—a move which his own transpositional logical operator precludes. A way out of this difficulty is not satisfactorily found by citing those texts in which he distinguishes between "being," "relative nonbeing," and "true nonbeing or nothingness." For, as will be clarified below, Nishida does not intend to *sublate* the thesis ("being") and the antithesis ("relative nonbeing") in a higher *dialectical synthesis* of "true nothingness." To the contrary, he rejects the identification of his logic of paradox with the logic of dialectical synthesis.

In the final analysis, then, "true nothingness" functions as a kind of shorthand expression of his *logic* of contradictory identity itself. It is to be returned to his *method* of articulation—his discursive pattern of categorial determination in the formal structure of mutual affirmation through mutual negation. In this semantic function, true "nothingness" is the logical matrix of the co-determination of binary opposites, another version of which takes the form of affirmation of the other through self-negation (and vice versa). The form is a symmetrical, but not sublational, one. It is a logic of the dynamic tension of opposites without higher synthesis, in the dyadic form of a mutual, or reciprocal, intentionality of opposing concepts. Nishida believed this "logic of nothingness" to be the "true logic." But even this is not quite true. He postulates a difference among logics—for example, the Aristotelian logic of the grammatical subject, the Kantian transcendental logic, and the Hegelian dialectical logic. His own logic is the logic of existential, religious self-consciousness. That is why it is the only "concrete logic," a phrase that is itself transparently paradoxical.

Nishida's "absolute nothingness" and related phrases will remain hopelessly elusive until we identify this specific semantic function of the logical operator in his text. The issue is comparable to his largely interchangeable usage of the terms "self" and "act." He tends to use "self" somewhat loosely in those passages where his fundamental metaphysical position is not at stake. But he switches to the more precise formulation of the unique "acts" of existential-historical consciousness when he is concerned with signifying that position. In contrast with this latter usage, "self" remains weighted with substantive, or noematic, connotations, although the notion of an enduring *eidos* or grammatical subject is repudiated by his finer analysis of the flux of "acts" as moments of world-realization. So too "nothingness" in its nominative usage remains a vague and misleading term until it is articulated—that is, translated—into the terms of his logic of contradictory identity.

Thus, perhaps a far more useful philosophical purpose is served when Nishida cites the "logic of *soku hi*" to elucidate his own concept of the "place of nothingness." *Soku hi*, the Japanese reading of the Chinese characters *chi fei*, or "is and is not," signifies the parity, and the structural biconditionality, of affirmative and negative. He illustrates this logical structure with the verse of the *Prajnaparamita Sutra* that reads: "Because there is no Buddha, there is Buddha, and because there are no sentient beings, there are sentient beings." Although mind-boggling to a first reader, Nishida's illustration is a crystal-clear expression of the logical form which we are pursuing in this analysis.[32]

Moreover, that Nishida's "absolute negation" is a shorthand expression of the paradoxical logic of contradictory identity is clear from the analogies to the Buddhist tradition that he draws out of the Western religious writers whom he frequently cites. Notable in this regard is his employment of the Christian theological concept of the divine *kenosis*. God's "emptying himself," he tells us, signifies precisely "God's creating and redeeming the world out of love." In numerous variations Nishida completes the biconditional structure of the *soku hi* paradox by arguing to the effect that it is equally true to say that the world's emptying itself signifies its creating and redeeming of God.[33]

It is also germane to take note of the fact that the precedent for this translation of the logic of nothingness into the more precise logic of *soku hi* is traceable to the *locus classicus* of Mahayana Buddhist hermeneutics—Nāgārjuna's correlation of "emptiness" *(sunyata)* with "dependent co-arising" *(pratitya samut-pada)*. Co-origination is the formal logical operator in Nāgārjuna's text.[34] And Nishida himself alludes explicitly to Nāgārjuna's Middle Path logic as a variant on the *soku hi* structure. He claims that Nāgārjuna's "negative theology" exhibits a version of the structure of the dynamic transposition of affirmative and negative. He makes the same point in reference to Nāgārjuna's table of the "eightfold negation," each of which is a subaltern form of the *soku hi* paradox.

Now all the forms of Mahayana Buddhism presuppose Nāgārjuna's logical hermeneutic, in Nishida's view. Therefore its cardinal teaching of the nonduality of nirvana and samsara can never be adequately framed in the dialectical language of Plato or Hegel. It is perhaps in this context that Nishida best clarifies the difference between sublational and paradoxical logical operators in his own mind. He also suggests, contrary to the standard dialectical articulations, that the Christian theology of the divine *kenosis* (or God's absolute self-negation as the form of his absolute love) is paradoxical in structure.[35] He follows Kierkegaard here. Neither concept, Buddhological or Christological, has anything to do with pantheism, in his understanding.

Pantheism, in Nishida's account, entails a substantive or noematic ontology—which he finds in the texts of Cusanus, Spinoza, and Hegel. At the same time, it tends to take a dialectical form of articulation—as in Cusanus or Hegel, though not Spinoza. Dialectical logic proceeds by the rubric of thesis, antithesis, and their resolution in a higher synthesis. Epistemologically, it is the method of discovering new and more inclusive ideas out of the clash of opposing, subaltern ideas—as in Plato's *Dialogues*. But ontologically, it is the method of the immanent unfoldment of an absolute subject—as in Hegel's *Phenomenology*. In contradistinction to this logic, Nishida maintains, the logic of paradox preserves the thesis and antithesis in tension. It has the biconditional structure of affirmation if, and only if, negation, and conversely of negation if, and only if, affirmation. He argues in this regard that the *Prajnaparamita Sutra* literature, the originating point of all Mahayana Buddhism, has a version of "the paradox of God" that cannot be reduced to dialectical, or pantheistic, terms.

In this context, therefore, the crux of the distinction between *dialectical* and *paradoxical* logical operators is that whereas the former exhibits the One returning to the One through the method of the negation of negation, the latter, the logic of *soku hi*, exhibits the dynamic tension of affirmative and negative without synthesis. Nishida's "place of nothingness" is more aptly rendered as the place of the paradoxical transposition of affirmative and negative in the self's own infinite depths. This existential "place" is the logical matrix of the co-origination of opposites —a paradoxical *coincidentia oppositorum* in the form of the mutual presence and absence of God and the self. Each self-conscious act of personal experience is this "place" of the absolute activity of concrete reality.

It should be noted that Nishida's text does not always clarify these distinctions, despite his intent to do so. He often employs the word "dialectical" *(benshōhōteki)* in conjunction with statements about his logic. It is the case, too, that his earlier writings adapt a generalized Hegelian language of the "concrete universal," and there are many instances of Nishida's predilection for a hierarchical ontology and axiology articulated in terms of "enveloping universals." Moreover, he adhered to Fichte's dialectical mode of articulation for ten years (from 1917 to 1927). In the mid-1930s he also thematized his philosophy in reference to the concept of "the world as dialectical universal." Only in the last ten years of his life did Nishida come to favor, and increasingly exhibit, the language of contradictory identity—literally, "the self-identity of absolute contradiction" *(zettai mujun no jiko dōitsu)*—as his logical operator. It is true that the word "dialectical" lingered on—as a kind of karmic residue in his mind and in his text—to the end of his career. Nevertheless, a significant feature of the "Religious Worldview" essay has to do with Nishida's sense of the difference between dialectical and paradoxical logics. In his view, the texts of Hegel and Marx represent a dialectical, sublational logic while those of Kierkegaard and Dostoievski represent versions of a paradoxical logic. Again, the texts of the Christian mystics and theologians, including Tillich, are sensemaking in dialectical form while Buddhist texts, in Nishida's understanding, have a paradoxical form of articulation.

Typically, Nishida cites the Christian Neo-Platonic mystics

and theologians Erigena, Eckhart, Boehme, and Cusanus in support of his own sense of the religious consciousness. But he always assimilates their respective doctrines into his own. He transmutes the dialectical form of their texts, which finally center on the doctrine of Christ, the mediating *Verbum*, into his own articulation of the contradictory identity of the absolute and the self. The Christological doctrine is replaced with a Buddhological one of an unmediated, nondual, co-originating identity. Moreover, while retaining the standard, but "unorthodox," Christian mystical principle of the absolute simultaneity and identity of God and the self, Nishida transforms its noumenal ontological sense into his own existential one. He does the same to the text of Schelling, which in all these semantic respects is isomorphic with the texts of Plotinus and the medieval Christian apophatic theologians.

Here we can say that Nishida's text has a special relation to Schelling's in that both writers effect transformations of Kantian and Fichtean positions within the transcendental language of those latter authors. Nishida agrees with Schelling in repudiating the Kantian and Fichtean principle of rational autonomy—pure reason legislating and positing its own forms in its own reflexive freedom—in favor of a "dark" principle of absolute Identity, or Indifference. Schelling's own principle of Identity as *Urgrund* or *Ungrund*, in its turn, drew explicitly upon Boehme's, among other apophatical mystical writers. Nishida agreed to that extent —and extended Schelling's critique of the rational principle to the texts of Hegel and Husserl, among others. But he transformed Schelling's dialectical articulation of the noumenal personality of God into his own paradoxically existential doctrine.

Evidence of these semantic transformations is ubiquitous in the "Religious Worldview" essay of 1945. As one example, let us cite this articulation of Nishida's position:

> The human self is individual as a self-negation of the absolute. But the more it is consciously self-forming through its own dynamic expression—that is, volitional and personal—the more it discovers its own absolute negation in its bottomlessly contradictory depths, and thus faces an absolute One—faces God as God's own mirror image and opposite. At the very root of our individuality we always face the absolute face of God, and stand in the dimension of decision between eternal life and death.

This passage is a clear expression of Nishida's existential sense of the contradictory identity of God and the self, a relation that is unmediated because it is paradoxically nondual. Nishida's text again shares with Schelling's a sense of the struggle between the forces of good and evil in the divine and human self. Both philosophers go so far as to say that God must in some essential respect be Satan, and that these opposing powers struggle on the battleground of the human heart. But he rejects Schelling's sense of a noumenal transmutation of the dark basis into light—a transmutation effected through the dialectically triumphant, spiritual principle in God. In that respect Nishida remained closer to Dostoievski, over against Schelling and the Christian mystics, in seeing the tensions of the human heart vanish, unmediated, into their own bottomlessly contradictory depths. In respect of Dostoievski, however, Nishida assimilated the Russian writer's subjective existentialism into his own Buddhist perspective, with its special "eschatological" sense of that vanishing point of the existential present that is the Dharmakaya itself.

A propos of the present point let me add here only one of many possible citations from the Zen master Dōgen, to show a structural, or eidetic, similarity with Nishida's form of expression. Dōgen writes in the chapter entitled *Menjū* ("Direct, Face to Face Transmission") of his masterwork, the *Shōbō genzō:*

> The interdependence between Buddha and ourselves cannot be measured. . . . Through our devotion to Shakyamuni's face, we will reflect his eye in our own. When this occurs it becomes Buddha's vision and original face. . . . If we transmit the right eye of the Law and venerate the Buddha, we become closer to him than he is to himself.[36]

Although Nishida does not cite this passage from Dōgen, he does highlight the concept of mutual encounter in passages drawn from several other Zen figures. He articulates the same metaphor by drawing on another, that of "inverse polarity" *(gyakutaiō)*, which he uses in nominative, adverbial, and adjectival forms. The *gyakutaiō* metaphor is illustrated in the passage above describing the existential self facing God as God's own *mirror image.*

Nishida was of course aware that in Leibniz's monadology could be found another foundational version of the mirror image.

Each of the monads is God's own expression in the perfect, preestablished calculus of the divine creative act. Each of the monads in turn expresses God, and through God, the entire universe. Characteristically, Nishida set out to transform Leibniz's meaning into his own. In Nishida's text, Leibniz's metaphysical monads become existential monads—a position that would indeed have appeared paradoxical to Leibniz. Nishida's 1944 essay, "Toward a Philosophy of Religion By Way of the Concept of Preestablished Harmony," looms in the background of the "Religious Worldview" essay. In its own modest way it is a small masterpiece of the assimilation of one philosopher's text by another's.

Now it will perhaps be helpful in this context to repeat that Nishida's concept of *gyakutaiō* has something in common with Kierkegaard's articulation of the "absolute paradox" of existential religious subjectivity. Nishida in fact refers approvingly to *Fear and Trembling* in his "Religious Worldview" essay. He was also familiar with Kierkegaard's *Concluding Unscientific Postscript*, which contains a clear patterning of this logic of "absolute paradox" in antagonism to the dialectical logic of Hegel.[37] What Kierkegaard says about the existential Christian self, who is established in the God-relationship by the risk of faith, is something Nishida himself discovers in Christianity. Conversely, Kierkegaard's articulation of "the Paradox of the eternal truth in time," and of the relation of the eternal truth and sinful human nature, is structurally affine to what Nishida finds in the Mahayana Buddhist tradition.

The value of taking note of this structural convergence in the thought of Nishida and Kierkegaard is that the latter's polemic in the nineteenth century against Kant's critical grounding of "science," and more pointedly against Hegel's dialectical articulation of "absolute science," provides an access to Nishida's own text as a whole, and especially to his elusive logical operator. If Kierkegaard's "absolute paradox" is openly antagonistic to Hegel's dialectical formulation, and Nishida's "logic" is isomorphic with Kierkegaard's, then Nishida's text will gain in clarity when it is seen as contributing its own version of this hermeneutical profile.[38] In a broader analysis, Nishida and Kierkegaard can be seen as contributing mutually enhancing versions of the paradoxical logical operator in philosophical texts.[39]

Nishida's text, we have seen, does not always clarify the distinction between paradoxical and dialectical logical operators which Kierkegaard's polemic against Hegel succeeds in setting in sharp relief. Nevertheless his "logic of nothingness" intends to be a version of this paradoxical logic. Perhaps Nishida's favorite illustration in this regard is the following passage from the Zen master Myōchō (Daitō Kokushi):

> Buddha and I, distinct through a billion kalpas of time,
> Yet not separate for a single instant;
> Facing each other the whole day through,
> Yet not facing each other for an instant.

Nishida returns to this passage in several places when he wants to exhibit fully his logic of mutual presence and absence in the existential dimension of "faith" or "enlightenment." In its structure, the verses well illustrate the symmetrical, and biconditional, character of his logical operator. Reduced to its essential factors, the relation between Buddha and self has the *form* of facing and yet not facing, not facing and yet facing—the *form* of simultaneous transcendence and immanence, immanence and transcendence. The circular character of this *soku hi* construction is not merely redundant, but serves to exhibit the dynamic equilibrium of opposites in this method of articulation.

Characteristically, however, Nishida chooses to illuminate a structural parallel to this Zen theme in the Western tradition. He cites Kierkegaard's *Fear and Trembling* on the point that Abraham's willingness to sacrifice Isaac has an entirely different significance than that of Agamemnon's sacrifice of Iphigenia.

> When Abraham took Isaac early in the morning to Mount Moria, he encountered God as the unique individual Abraham, a sheer human being, the ultimate point of real humanity. God called out, "Abraham." And he answered, "Behold, I am here."

God then blessed Abraham for honoring his word. To Nishida, the crux of this episode lies in the existential, face to face encounter between God and the self-conscious Abraham. His interpretation of "faith" and the "Word" of God is consistent with this paradoxical articulation of the ontological co-determination of God and the self. We can say that Nishida's thought acknowledges the resonance between Zen and Kierkegaardian concepts in this instance.[40]

"The Logic of the Place of Nothingness and the Religious Worldview" may thus impress the reader as a powerful hermeneutic of both religious traditions, East and West. Nishida is perhaps the first of the world-theologians of our times. He does not merely represent the East when he enters into a dialogue with Kierkegaard, Barth, Tillich, and the other Western theologians whom he cites. Nishida is as much a biblical or Christian theologian as he is a Buddhist theologian when he turns to the sacred texts of religion. But in the final analysis, his global theological insight is grounded in the methodological procedure of his own text. The "Religious Worldview" essay is a good example of the role a philosophical hermeneutic can play in theological interpretation.

Now if both premodern and modern Japanese civilization has been distinguished for its syncretic features, Nishida's text is an outstanding reflection of this tendency as well. This aspect of his writings is reminiscent of such great Japanese syncretists as Kūkai, Dōgen, and Ikkyū. Among Nishida's immediate predecessors in the twentieth century there are such figures as Natsume Sōseki and Mori Ōgai, two towering writers who pursue intercivilizational themes in literary forms. In the broader philosophical context, Nishida's global hermeneutic merits consideration in the company of such great architectonic philosophers of the West as Aristotle, Leibniz, Kant, Hegel, and Whitehead. His religious worldview may be, to date, without a contemporary peer in providing a cross-cultural mapping of the religious and philosophical structures of East and West. It merits, at the very least, a critical analysis, with an eye to developing a more complete mapping of the East-West domain.

Be that as it may, a significant feature of Nishida's text is that its own hermeneutical profile provides a structural access to the variety of premodern texts he cites. With its numerous allusions to the Mahayana Buddhist tradition alone, "The Logic of the Place of Nothingness and the Religious Worldview" is plainly Nishida's own endeavor to provide such a hermeneutic. In the wider framework to which I am alluding, Nishida's text appears to have the same eidetic profile as such prototypical Ch'an texts as *The Platform Sutra of the Sixth Patriarch* and *The Record of Lin-chi.* Essential features of this thought pattern can be traced in Japanese Buddhist figures such as Dōgen and Ikkyū as well. Each of these texts and authors offers a version of a hermeneutical profile which can be characterized as exhibiting an existentialist ontological focus, a paradoxical logic, and a consummatory intention of the active self-realization of the Buddha-nature. What is significant here is that Nishida's version of this profile breaks out of the sectarian confines of Buddhist thought and practice to achieve its status as a form of world philosophy.

We have seen that Nishida's logic underlies his critique of the religious consciousness, and that both logic and critique subtend his religious worldview. He argues that the true God must possess himself in self-negation. It is for this same reason that we exist as the self-negations of God—we are "images of God" as God's self-reflections. Nishida has thus drawn a fine but decisive line between his thought and that of Hegel. While Hegel's principle is the self-reflective character of the divine Reason and his method of articulation is dialectical, Nishida's principle is that of absolute identity and his method is paradoxical. And while Hegel's ontological focus consists in the universal, recurrent forms of logical, natural, and historical being, Nishida's sense of reality centers on the existential monads, each of which functions as an absolutely discontinuous "act" of world-realization. The religious self finds itself only by losing itself in the "vanishing point" of its own active intuition.

Nishida rings a number of changes, Christian and Buddhist, on these traditional expressions to articulate the religious form of life. The religious "act" of self-awareness is the place of realization of the coincidence of eternal life and death in one's own life and death. To fathom this paradoxical *coincidentia oppositorum* in one's own religious awareness is to experience an authentic "conversion," whether in Christian or Buddhist terms. It is impossible, Nishida says, to conceive of this religious metanoesis in the Aristotelian terms of substance logic or in the Kantian framework of moral self-power. The dynamics of religious conversion entail the reciprocal, but nondual, intentionality of God and the individual soul. "Faith" and "grace" are names for this dimension of mutual, and transpositional, revealment. They are existential modes of realization of "the absolute present" in which, Nishida says, "in the bottomless depths of the self there is that which transcends the self and from which the self is to be conceived."

The mutual presence and absence, immanence and transcendence, of God and the self thus becomes for Nishida the logical form in which to repossess hermeneutically the Mahayana concept of the nonduality of samsara and nirvana. He explores several Zen versions of this theme in his essay's recurring motif of enlightenment as the "ordinary and everyday." The historical-existential self in this religious dimension of self-awareness is described by Nishida as having an "eschatological" character, based on its *"absolute freedom"* as the self-negation of God. In this context, Nishida's espousal of the Ch'an master Lin-chi's doctrine of absolute freedom, at the expense of Kant's concept of *moral* freedom, is another instance of his shift in method and ontological focus in respect of Kant's position. Nishida also pursues this point in reference to Tillich's *Kairos und Logos.*

Nishida returns in several places to the theme of God or Buddha as absolute love and infinite compassion. The true God, he argues, must paradoxically negate himself even to the extent of being Satan. He finds here the religious significance of the concept of "expedient means" *(upaya),* which is intrinsically linked to the Mahayana logic of the nonduality of samsara and nirvana. He also discovers here the logical basis of Shinran's teaching that "the evil man is the true cause of Amida's vow." And in Christianity, too, the kenotic theology of the Cross vividly expresses the logic of the absolute self-negation of God. The biblical Word of God and the Pure Land Buddhist concept of "calling the name of Amida" *(myōgō)* become other instances of Nishida's understanding of the religious encounter as entailing "the absolutely contradictory identity of God and man."

Now in his endeavor to provide a critique of the religious consciousness Nishida highlights the fact that religious conversion and religious experience have an active character. From his earliest writings he had explored the concept of the religious form of life as entailing "the value of the negation of value." The sacred, he also says, arises "in the direction of the transcendence of value." This is because real value must be grounded in active self-existence, which paradoxically involves an absolute other. It involves God's grace and Buddha's compassion, in conjunction with a total religious exertion.

The active character of this religious transvaluation signifies for Nishida that an authentic conversion occurs in a dimension of "spirituality" that has nothing to do with subjective peace of mind. It involves an "absolute overturning" of the grammatical subject and predicate standpoints of the self. Consequently such an overturning—what in Yogacara Buddhism is termed a "revolution in the personality base"—cannot be understood as a processive attainment by virtue of the self's own power.[41] For the religious self cannot remove its own existential contradiction. (Nor can the moral self.) We are intrinsically sinners and deluded, and there must be, in Shinran's phrase, "an overleaping way to salvation." The "deliverance" in the conversion experience entails the self-negation of the divine—the dynamism of God's love or the Buddha's compassion—and simultaneously, the self-negation of the existential self in its metanoesis.

The active character of the conversion experience therefore exhibits a transpositional structure: the self-negation of the self and the self-negation of the divine, in that matrix of mutual encounter called "faith" or "enlightenment." In one passage Nishida juxtaposes Luther's teaching with Zen to bring this out. He cites Luther to the effect that "faith" is the working of God within us; we are newly made to live by God, we kill the old Adam, and we become entirely other persons, accompanied by the Holy Spirit. Zen "enlightenment" speaks of "seeing into one's own nature and thus becoming the Buddha-nature." This "seeing" is similarly not to be construed one-sidedly, either as a transcendent, noematic intention or as an immanent, noetic act. It is rather a total overturning of the self, an opening up of its existential depths at the vanishing point of its contradictory identity as a self-determination of the absolute present. "Faith" and "enlightenment" are overturning experiences precisely in the interplay of these transformative forces through which God/Buddha and the self face each other across the infinite abyss of life and death.

Nishida's metalogical elaborations thus allow him to highlight significant structural relations among Western and Eastern religious traditions. Christianity, he notes, places the origin of religion in man's fall through the original sin of Adam. Sinners by birth, we have no way to escape from the side of man. God sends his only begotten son to redeem the world out of his infinite love. We are saved by conversion to and faith in the redemptive act of Christ. Nishida comments here that the concept of original sin is an extremely irrational idea as an *ethical* doctrine. And yet it expresses a fundamental fact of human life.

This religious fact finds another expression in the teaching of the True Pure Land school of Mahayana Buddhism, which similarly rejects the ethical way of moral self-power. It also teaches that we are intrinsically sinful, and that we are saved only through the other-power of Amida's infinite compassion. In either Christian or Pure Land form, religious conversion signifies penetrating to that self-contradictory depth of the self from which saving graces flood in. Nishida even relates Dōgen's statement that "to study the way of Buddha is to study the self, and to study the self is to forget the self" to this cross-cultural pattern. He claims that Christian, Pure Land, and Zen versions of religious practice, while differing in institutional and rhetorical symbols, share a common logical structure as they respectively repudiate every religion of self-power. The essential mark of their praxis is found in the dynamics of self-cultivation through self-negation in which an "overleaping way to salvation" is opened up.

Another salient aspect of Nishida's critique of the religious consciousness is his insistence on religious individuality. Already adumbrated in his citation of Pascal's "thinking reed" metaphor, religious individuality entails that existential self-awareness of a *being* facing its own eternal *nothingness*. But in fact each act of consciousness reveals one's life and one's death. The more a person achieves self-awareness in the act as a unique determination of the absolute present, the more that person acts as a dynamic expression of the historical world.

The historical (that is, personal, human) world is a movement from the created form to the creating form: and this is exemplified in the transforming expression of religious individuality. The more a person becomes religiously volitional, taking the risk of faith in Kierkegaard's sense, the more he faces an absolute other and simultaneously opens himself up to the working of

God or Buddha within himself. But this opening is a mutual opening—a co-originative event. This is the philosophical meaning of Dōgen's *genjō kōan:* the paradox *(kōan)* of the presencing of the Buddha-nature and simultaneously of subjective, existential realization *(genjō).*

Nishida therefore writes: "In any religion . . . gaining religious faith must proceed from the well-sharpened edge of the consciously active, individual will." Religion does not proceed from mere emotion. It involves the "total exertion of the self"—as witnessed in the many Zen expressions he cites which illustrate his own existential principle. To Nishida there cannot be anything like an aesthetic religion. Art and religion represent two opposing directions in this respect. Creative individuality in its religiously volitional (but not moral self-power) character is again grounded by Nishida in his metaphysics of the existential self-determination of the absolute present. He juxtaposes teachings taken from Zen and Pure Land Buddhism to bring this out. Lin-chi's "In this mass of red flesh there abides the True Man of No Rank: he constantly exits and enters through your own face" and Shinran's "When I deeply reflect upon Amida's vow which he contemplated for five kalpas of time, I find that it was for the sake of myself alone, Shinran" are both interpreted by Nishida as instances of his concept of sheer religious individuality. But characteristically he also turns here to Kierkegaard, to bring out the difference between morality (which is universal) and religion (which is individual). Nishida agrees with Kierkegaard that the "moral knight" and the "knight of faith" stand in mutually contradictory dimensions.

The religiously active individual therefore encounters God or Buddha in the intimately personal dimension of interexpression through mutual affirmation and negation. "The self faces the absolute at the limit point of its own individual will. God, too, faces the self in his absolute will." Active religious expression must be ec-static—a leap of faith in that existential dimension wherein the act is the contradictory identity of transcendent and immanent planes of self-awareness. The act always has the paradoxical form of active intuition. Toward the conclusion of his essay Nishida writes that the perfect expression of this religious form of self-awareness is found in Shinran's statement: "My pronouncing the name of Amida is also the design of Amida himself." The reader will perhaps feel that Nishida cites these words of Shinran to express what is contained in the depths of his own soul. They are the profoundly personal words of religious faith of the seventy-five-year-old philosopher.

Notes

1. *Nishida Kitarō zenshū* (The Collected Works of Nishida Kitarō), 2d ed., 19 vols. (Tokyo: Iwanami Shoten, 1965). Hereafter cited as *NKZ.*

2. The case of Mori Ōgai's career is particularly revealing of the intercivilizational thrust of modern Japanese culture in the Meiji and Taisho eras in which Nishida himself grew to philosophical maturity. See David A. Dilworth, "The Significance of Ōgai's Historical Literature," in *Saiki Kōi and Other Stories: The Historical Literature of Mori Ōgai* (Honolulu: University Press of Hawaii, 1977), 1–31.

3. He first began to formulate this concept in 1927 by reconstructing his own earlier versions of "pure experience," "intuition," and "self-consciousness" drawn from such authors as William James, Bergson, and Fichte. The prevailing focus of Nishida's pre-1927 philosophical thought can be traced in his *A Study of Good* (1911) and *Thought and Experience* (1915), which show the influence of James and Bergson; and in *Intuition and Reflection in Self-consciousness* (1917), *Problems of Consciousness* (1920), and *Art and Morality* (1923), which proceed to reformulate his earlier position in cognizance of the doctrines of Kant and various Neo-Kantians, Husserl, and especially Fichte. After 1927, Nishida produced various formulations of his master-concept of "absolute nothingness" *(zettai mu)* in four new works: *From Acting to Seeing* (1927), *The Self-conscious System of the Universal* (1930), *The Self-conscious Determination of Nothingness* (1932), and *Fundamental Problems of Philosophy* (1933–34, in two volumes).

4. Notably in "Toward a Philosophy of Religion By Way of the Concept of Preestablished Harmony" (1944), and "The Logic of the Place of Nothingness and the Religious Worldview" (1945). It is important to note that these two essays come at the end of the six volumes of Nishida's *Tetsugaku rombunshū* (Philosophical Essays) written between 1935 and 1945. This last phase of Nishida's career represents one of the most productive phases of his thought. In these six volumes there are twenty-eight essays, totaling over fifteen hundred pages in the standard edition of Nishida's Collected Works (*NKZ* 8–11).

5. In Husserl, the transcendental domain is a pure field of subjectivity conditioned by an "I think." *Transcendent* objects within the empiri-

cal domain appear as objects of consciousness when constituted phenomenologically in the *transcendental* field. Kant's own use of these terms is tied to his synoptic, as distinguished from phenomenological, method of articulation of the essential parts of pure reason into their theoretical and practical uses. Nishida favored Husserl's formulation because of the latter's project of overcoming Kant's appearance/reality dichotomy. In the final analysis, however, Nishida's text is existentialist in its ontological focus whereas Husserl's is essentialist. We shall explore these hermeneutical distinctions in the body of the present Introduction.

6. See the masterful exposition of Nishida's argument in *The Self-conscious System of the Universal* (1930) in Robert J. J. Wargo, *The Logic of Basho and the Concept of Nothingness in the Philosophy of Nishida Kitarō* (Ann Arbor: University Microfilms International, 1972), 174–361.

7. During this last phase of Nishida's thinking, the philosophy of Hegel played a constant formative role. But Nishida's text represents a deliberate shift in the method of its own internal discursive operation. Over against Hegel's dialectical logic, it adopts a paradoxical form of categorial determination; and it does so in respect of an existential ontological sense of the formative acts of world-realization that represents another departure from Hegel's text.

8. The title of *Bashoteki ronri to shūkyōteki sekaikan* translates literally as "The Logic of Place and the Religious Worldview." But it will be seen that the "logic of place" is itself multivariable, involving several matrices *(basho)* of transcendental analysis. This accounts, I believe, for Nishida's otherwise vague use of *bashoteki* in the title itself. For the purposes of an English translation "the logic of place" (or of *locus, topos*) falls short of adequate philosophical connotation. I have therefore rendered the title as "The Logic of the Place *of Nothingness,*" to establish continuity with other articulations of Nishida's doctrine, such as *The Self-conscious Determination of Nothingness* (1932); this usage accords with existing English translations—for example, Robert Schinzinger's translation of *Intelligibility and the Philosophy of Nothingness* (Honolulu: East-West Center Press, 1958)—and provides a more explicit reference to the foundational doctrine of Nishida's work.

9. *Watakushi no ronri ni tsuite* (Concerning My Logic), *NKZ* 12:265–67; see the translation below, pp. 125–126.

10. Immanuel Kant, *Critique of Practical Reason*, trans. Lewis White Beck (New York: Bobbs-Merrill, 1956), 167.

11. Immanuel Kant, *Critique of Pure Reason*, trans. F. Max Müller (New York: Anchor Books, 1966), 17–18, 530–540.

12. Lewis White Beck, "Translator's Introduction," in Kant, *Critique of Practical Reason*, x.

13. Kant's explicit employment of Plato's concepts is found in the

Critique of Practical Reason, for example on pp. 43–51, as well as *passim* in the writings of his critical period.

14. *Critique of Practical Reason,* 133–36.

15. *Ibid.,* 10 (Kant's emphasis).

16. *Ibid.,* 33.

17. *Ibid.*

18. *Ibid.,* 86.

19. *Ibid.,* 87.

20. *Ibid.,* 125.

21. *Ibid.,* 127–28.

22. *Ibid.,* 111.

23. *Ibid.,* 6.

24. *Ibid.,* 166.

25. It should be clear that Kant's noumenal definition of the domain of pure practical reason radically differentiates his grounding of the science of morals from that of Aristotle. The Greek philosopher's eudaimonic principle of "happiness" as the controlling *telos* of the acquirement and the activity of the moral life is thus constantly under attack in Kant's text, as are all other groundings of morals (for example, of Hume, of the Stoics and Epicureans, of Spinoza, among others).

26. Leibniz's position is ubiquitously articulated in his philosophical essays and correspondence. See the representative texts in Philip P. Weiner, ed., *Leibniz: Selections* (New York: Scribners, 1951), 90–280. A focused discussion of Leibniz's same views is found in John Herman Randall, *The Career of Philosophy,* vol. 2 (New York: Columbia University Press, 1965), 19–28.

27. The author is indebted to Patrick A. Milburn for the language of some of these formulations.

It is perhaps instructive to note here that Nishida's method of articulation (through the transpositional language of the mutual contradiction of opposites) diverges from the logistic (quantitatively incremental) method of articulation in Darwin's *Origin of Species.* Darwin's text follows Democritus (and Newton), moreover, in respect of its substrative ontological focus (namely, the material reality of the "species") while Nishida's focus is existential. Because of his focus on humanly self-conscious awareness, Nishida does not pursue, as does Darwin, the concept of universal forms in embodied organisms, along the lines of a general theory of the mutations of organisms or of species. He rather tends to subsume the universal-particular relationships exhibited in the biological world under the rubric of his transpositional language of contradictory identity, while shifting the "real" signification of his ontology—what he calls "concrete" as opposed to abstract—to the existentially unique "acts of consciousness" of the human world.

28. According to Nishida, his essay on the I-Thou relation, which he penned toward the end of his *Self-conscious Determination of Nothingness* in 1932, represents a critical juncture in the development of his thought. He thematized the I-Thou relation thereafter in various contexts. See *NKZ* 6:341ff.

29. In Kant, "the concept of the highest good" entails a precise transcendental analysis of pure practical reason. The concept has two parts, which are correlated as ground and consequent. The former is the concept of moral worthiness, grounded in the autonomous activity of the moral will itself, and the latter is the concept of happiness, in the sense of just reward (in the next life) for one's moral worth. This concept of the highest good, with its religious postulates, subtends Kant's articulations of his "pure rational faith" in the second *Critique* and of his "moral theology" in his third *Critique*. See Kant's *Critique of Practical Reason*, 114-15, 128-36, and *passim*; and *Critique of Judgment*, trans. J. H. Bernard (New York: Hafner, 1951), 312-26 and *passim*.

30. See "Postscript: Nishida's Logic of the East," pp. 127-149 below, for further discussion of these claims.

31. While Nishida does not refer in this context to Nicolas of Cusa's *De Docta Ignorantia*, we know from other sources that he felt a close affinity to the German theologian's formulations. It would appear that Nishida is drawing directly on Cusanus' doctrine that God, the Absolute or Maximum, is "opposed to nothing," while at the same time assimilating the Christian Neo-Platonic theological framework into his own. On this concept of the Absolute's being "opposed to nothing," cf. *De Docta Ignorantia*, bk. 1, chaps. 2 and 5, in Jasper Hopkins, *Nicholas of Cusa on Learned Ignorance: A Translation and an Appraisal of De Docta Ignorantia* (Minneapolis: Banning Press, 1981), 51ff., 55ff.

32. It is interesting to see that Plato's *Parmenides* attempts a rather comprehensive mapping of the grammatological possibilities of "is" and "is not" at a "hypothetical" level of analysis of metaphysical discourse. See David A. Dilworth, "Nāgārjuna's *Catuṣkoṭikā* and Plato's *Parmenides*. Grammatological Mappings of a Common Textual Form," *Journal of Buddhist Philosophy* 2 (1984): 77-104.

33. In this respect we are reminded of the ostensibly paradoxical formulation of Whitehead in the concluding pages of *Process and Reality:*

> It is as true to say that God is permanent and the World fluent, as that the World is permanent and God is fluent.
> It is as true to say that God is one and the World many, as that the World is one and God many.
> It is as true to say that, in comparison with the World, God is actual

> eminently, as that, in comparison with God, the World is actual eminently.
>
> It is as true to say that the World is immanent in God, as that God is immanent in the World.
>
> It is as true to say that God transcends the World, as that the World transcends God.
>
> It is as true to say that God creates the World, as that the World creates God.

See Alfred North Whitehead, *Process and Reality* (New York: Harper and Row, 1960), 528. But such ostensible parallels among philosophical forms of discourse only point up the hermeneutical problem. The question is finally one of the exact nodes of convergence and divergence of the semantic presuppositions of texts. In a hermeneutical analysis, I would submit, Whitehead's text presupposes a dialectical form of articulation, as distinguished from the paradoxical form of Nishida's text.

For another example, the Christian mystic Angelus Silesius writes:

> I know God cannot live a moment without me;
> If I should come to nought, He too must cease to be.

This passage, from Silesius' *Cherubinischer Wandersmann,* is cited in Arthur Schopenhauer, *The World as Will and Representation,* vol. 1, trans. F. J. Payne (New York: Dover, 1969), 129. This text will also be seen to presuppose a dialectical form of articulation, although Nishida would proceed to understand it in a paradoxical form.

34. The logic of Nāgārjuna as providing the Buddhological background of the texts of Nishida and of Nishitani Keiji is elaborated by Hans Waldenfels in his *Absolute Nothingness: Foundations of a Buddhist-Christian Dialogue,* trans. J. W. Heisig (New York: Paulist Press, 1980), 15–23 and *passim.* This logical structure is fully exhibited, in numerous variations, in Nishitani's *Religion and Nothingness,* trans. Jan Van Bragt (Los Angeles: University of California Press, 1982). In addition to Nishitani's text, see also the entries in Van Bragt's glossary under "sive" *(soku)* and *sive/non (soku hi),* and Van Bragt's further references in chap. 5, n. 19, p. 291.

35. Nishida's various formulations of this point would appear to be a major source of the interpretive assimilation of the kenotic theology of the Cross in the encounter theology of the Kyoto School. This persistent theme can be traced, for example, in the writings of Nishitani Keiji, Hisamatsu Shin'ichi, Takeuchi Yoshinori, and Abe Masao, as listed by Waldenfels in the bibliography of *Absolute Nothingness.* The standard Kyoto School articulation, stemming from that of Nishida, tends to sup-

press the "And God shall exalt Him" conclusion of Philippians 2. The Kyoto School does this because of its own doctrinal presupposition; it is being true to the existential signification of Buddhist discourse. This amounts to a reordering of the metaphysical priority of the evangelical text, which itself is noumenal in ontological focus (Christ's kingdom is not of this world, Christ's resurrection, and exaltation). Waldenfel's *Absolute Nothingness* touches upon this point in various contexts.

36. Dōgen Zenji, *Shōbōgenzō: The Eye and the Treasury of the True Law*, trans. Kōsen Nishiyama and John Stevens, 2 vols. (Tokyo: Nakayama Shobō, 1975, 1977), 2:138.

37. Soren Kierkegaard, *Concluding Unscientific Postscript*, trans. David F. Swenson and Walter Lowrie (Princeton: Princeton University Press, 1941), 140–219, 313–16, and *passim*.

38. Kierkegaard's "unscientific" attitude is met forthwith in the preface to *Fear and Trembling*. See *Kierkegaard's Writings*, vol. 6, ed. and trans. Howard V. Hong and Edna H. Hong (Princeton: Princeton University Press, 1983), 7. For Hegel's conception of a single body of philosophical science, which he called *The Encyclopaedia of the Philosophical Sciences*, see J. B. Baillie's introduction to G. W. F. Hegel, *The Phenomenology of Mind* (New York: Harper Books, 1967), 37–38.

39. This is an obvious context in which to note that Nishida's theme of religious individuality, which transcends the rational universal of the moral consciousness (as in Kant, Fichte, and Hegel), runs in tandem with Kierkegaard's vivid theme to the same effect in *Fear and Trembling*; see pp. 54ff.

40. In a final hermeneutical analysis, Kierkegaard's text will be seen as extremely unorthodox within the mainstreams of Christian religiosity. It is creative in its integrative assumption, paradoxical in method of articulation, noumenal in ontological signification, and subjective in perspective. It therefore also differs from that of Nishida or the Zen masters in two essential respects—in integrating principle and in perspective —thus producing its own unique profile of religious expression.

41. On the concept of "revolution in the personality base" *(asraya paravrtti)*, see Nagao Gadjin, "On the Theory of the Buddha-Body *(Buddha-kaya)*," trans. Umeyo Hirano, *The Eastern Buddhist*, n.s. 6, no. 1 (May 1973): 45–53. It is the Yogacara Buddhist tradition's version of diaphanic metanoesis, involving the transition from a former avidyic *episteme* to the enlightened *episteme*.

The Logic of the Place of Nothingness and the Religious Worldview

1

Not everyone is an artist. But to some extent at least everyone can appreciate art. Nor is everyone a theologian, and rare is the man who experiences a religious conversion. To some degree, however, any person can understand religion. There is probably no one who does not feel a strong resonance in the depths of his heart when he reads the fervent confessions of faith of those who have gained religious faith or the expressions of belief of the great religious figures. Moreover, upon falling into a condition of extreme unhappiness, there is probably no one who does not feel some religious sentiment welling up from the depths of his own soul.

For religion is an event of the soul. Philosophers cannot fabricate religion from their own thought systems. They must explain this event of the soul. To do so, they must experience religious sentiment in themselves to some degree.

Granting that the man of religion speaks from true personal experience, I will contend that just as people who are not artists appreciate art to some extent, so too ordinary people know what is meant by religion. There is no one who will declare that he has no conscience. If there were such a person he would in fact be engaging in a form of self-insult. There are people, however, who say they do not appreciate art; and especially in the case of religion, many insist they cannot understand it. They declare that they have no experience of a religious kind. Indeed, some philosophers even pride themselves in taking a contrary position. Religion, they say, is unscientific and illogical, or at most something subjectively mystical. Or they contend it is not that man is created in the image of God, but rather that God has been created in the image of man. Religion, we are told, is a kind of narcotic.

Now one cannot discuss colors with a blind man or discuss sounds with a deaf man. If people say they do not understand religion at all, I cannot argue with them. However, even though I do not consider myself competent to speak about religion to others, I cannot follow those who say they do not understand religion because it is unscientific and illogical. I hope in what follows to clarify at least that much.

Before discussing particular topics, I will clarify what I take religion to be. And this will entail an explanation of what I mean by religious sentiment. Religion is about God. God is fundamental to religion in any form. And just as color appears to the eye as color, and sound to the ear as sound, so too God appears to the religious self as an event of one's own soul. It is not a matter of God being conceivable or not conceivable in merely intellectual terms. What can be conceived or not conceived is not God.

And yet God cannot therefore be said to be a merely subjective experience of the soul. Truth in physics begins from sensory experience. That which sees and hears is not an organic sense organ such as the eye or ear, but the mind which knows physical phenomena objectively. Before articulating the a priori grounds of an ethical act in his *Kritik der praktischen Vernunft* Kant first discusses, in his *Grundlegung*, the meaning of the moral good in terms of ordinary ethical reasoning. I have nothing to add to Kant's formulation since it well clarifies what is ordinarily meant by the moral consciousness. Having such a clear understanding of the objective ground of morality, Kant proceeds to probe its subjective ground from the standpoint of his transcendental philosophy. Concerning the ordinary aesthetic consciousness, however, how well did Kant truly grasp it? His view that beauty is a feeling of disinterestedness—as is illustrated in Goethe's declaration that the stars in the heavens that are not objects of desire are most beautiful—cannot help being worthy of respect as a position that well clarifies the a priori grounds of a judgment of aesthetic appreciation. But does Kant's third *Kritik* define anything over and above mere formal beauty?

These considerations are to me relevant to the question of religion. It appears that Kant considered religion solely from the

standpoint of the transcendental moral consciousness. He regards
the immortality of the soul and the existence of God as mere postulates of the formal ethical will. To Kant, religion has significance as a vehicle that supplements morality. I cannot find in
Kant any autonomy given to the religious consciousness itself.
Perhaps he never even considered religion as an autonomous
sphere. I contend, however, that the religious form of life does not
fall within the sphere of mere reason, *blosse Vernunft.* That is
why one who discusses religion must experience, to some extent
at least, religious sentiment as an event of his own soul. If he does
not, then even if he intends to discuss religion he may in fact end
up talking about something else.

What, then, does the religious consciousness, or religious
sentiment, involve? This question must be deeply fathomed in
both its subjective and its objective senses. I cannot enter into
such an extensive study here. I will maintain, though, that the
subject of religious experience cannot be properly discussed from
the standpoint of reason with its logic of objects. Indeed, the
question of religion does not even arise from that standpoint. It
arises rather with a consideration of the meaning of our own consciously active self, and it leads us through and beyond the framework of Kant's transcendental definitions.

What does it mean to be a consciously active self? I hold that
the self is consciously active when it is interactive, and its
interactivity is constituted in a dialectic of mutual negation and
affirmation of self and other. Self and other, subject and object, are
constituted in the individual acts of existential consciousness.
These acts are self-originating and yet co-originating, too, as
forms of dynamic, reciprocal expression. It is in this structure of
biconditional, interexpressive, mutual revealment of self and
other that an individual act is an individual act.

One can first try to conceive of a world of interactive things
in the framework of the physical world. But here, already, we
promptly feel the need to work out a logic of dynamic, reciprocal
expression. For properly speaking, there is no real interactivity at
this level. Description in terms of the mere opposition, the action
and reaction, of physical entities falls considerably short of interactivity as dynamic, reciprocal expression. A truly active, and
consciously active, being is not merely moved by another, is not

something merely acted upon; it must equally move the other through itself, and be active from itself. As Leibniz puts it, we cannot even conceive of active beings in the physical world if it is reduced to spatial extensiveness, a world of merely quantitative forces.

The concept of a truly active being, to paraphrase Leibniz again, requires us to introduce the concept of order, and at the very least, of continuity. This further entails a concept of irreversible time. In the physical world time can be thought of as reversible; in the biological world, time is irreversible. Each pulsation of life is a unique event in time, which is an order of duration. Each pulsation of life, each formation of life, perishes, while the organism or the biological world endures. In this fashion the biological world is always moving, from the formed to the forming, within the structure of the contradictory identity of the many and the one. It is an infinite process of transformation. Living beings are dynamically formative, organic. That is why the biological world is conceivable in teleological terms.

In another essay, on "Life," I probed the difference between the physical and biological worlds on this basis. The latter exhibits this principle of self-expression; it reflects itself within itself. I articulate this difference by defining the biological world as a self-transforming matrix moving from the formed to the forming, through the dynamic transactions of organism and environment. The organic realm constitutes a world that exists and moves through itself in this way. It is a process of infinite transformation through the dynamic equilibrium of organism and environment—that is, it contains its own self-negation and self-affirmation within itself. This self-vectorial process constitutes the direction of time.

The biological world thus has the form of a contradictory identity, possessing its own organic centers within itself and infinitely determining itself in and through these centers. The emergence of new life presupposes that organic beings are active in this dynamic world through their mutual negation and affirmation. Each new pulsation of life is a vector of the biological world's own self-formation. It is in this sense that activity in the biological world entails direction. The temporal event must carry its own content; and a temporal vector must be conceived of as teleological.

Needless to say, we cannot even conceive of the physical world without presupposing some concept of time. Without it there can be no real meaning to the concept of force. However, in the physical world time is still predominantly spatial, something that has a self-negating character, whereas in the biological world every living being is an organic center of a self-forming world, as indicated above.

Having bodies, we, the human kind, are also biological beings and are active accordingly—we act teleologically in the character of our species. But we do not merely act teleologically, or socio-specifically. We act in our human-historical individuality, with individual purpose and self-awareness—individuality that has the structure of the absolutely contradictory identity of the many and the one. The biological and physical worlds always appear as subaltern dimensions of our own contradictory individuality. And though the biological world exhibits its own form of contradictory identity, it is still predominantly linked to the spatial, or physical, world even while it is enfolded in our own self-conscious historical individuality.

I say, then, that the human-historical world exhibits true, existential individuality through its structure of absolutely contradictory identity. This ultimately consists in the fact that each individual conscious act is a contradictory identity. For while the act exists and moves in itself, it dynamically expresses the world. In human consciousness, therefore, the world exhibits both a spatial and a temporal character. As an order of simultaneous existence it appears as a form of self-negation, and yet it is infinitely occurring in its temporality. Affirming itself in its temporality, it transcends its own spatial character by being a creative transformation.

Now time is the order of duration and succession while space is the order of simultaneous existence. In human consciousness the world is bottomlessly self-determining and creative, a transformational process which has the form of the contradictory identity of space and time. I refer to this self-forming, creative world as the self-determination of the absolute present. I hold that it is only in this dynamic form of contradictory identity that we can truly conceive of something that moves by itself and is self-conscious. The dynamic reciprocity of objective and subjective dimensions comprising the act of humanly conscious expression is monadological in this existential sense. It is unintelligible as the mere action and reaction of physical objects (that is, as grammatical subjects in the framework of theoretical judgment). It must be the expression of a self-determining and self-conscious act that simultaneously reflects the world as a unique perspective of the world.

When I say that the consciously active individual exists in a structure of dynamic expression, I mean precisely this. That I am consciously active means that I determine myself by expressing the world in myself. I am an expressive monad of the world. I transform the world into my own subjectivity. The world that, in its objectivity, opposes me is transformed and grasped symbolically in the forms of my own subjectivity. But this transactional logic of contradictory identity signifies as well that it is the world that is expressing itself in me. The world creates its own space-time character by taking each monadic act of consciousness as a unique position in the calculus of its own existential transformation. Conversely, the historical act is, in its space-time character, a self-forming vector of the world. To bring this out I say that the temporal-spatial (that is, conscious-spatial) reflects itself within itself as a contradictory identity. In this way each act of consciousness is a self-perspective of the dynamic, spatial-temporal world.

It is in this transpositional form that our worlds of consciousness construct the world's order and continuity. The existential act is always teleologically self-conscious as a temporal occurrence. It is so as a self-determining act of the world that transforms itself by expressing itself as the present which determines itself as the meeting point of past and future. Our conscious worlds are the places in which we express the world in ourselves as the contradictory identity of the transcendent and the immanent, of space and time. But as this contradictory identity that is constitutive of the act of consciousness itself, we are only active as formative positions in the world's own calculus of self-expression.

I have articulated this point in various writings. Expression entails the contradictory identity, and dynamic transaction, of the conscious act (self) and the world (other). Each conscious act is an existential monad of the world's own self-reflection. Our self-consciousness does not take place in a merely closed up, windowless self. It consists in the fact that the self, by transcending itself, faces and expresses the world. When we are self-conscious, we are already self-transcending. But such an evident truth has no place in a philosophy that substantializes the self and the act through some dogmatism based on object logic.

In the humanly conscious world having this structure of contradictory identity, self-consciousness is always interexpressive: world faces world, monad mirrors monad. In Leibniz's own terms, each monad expresses the world and simultaneously is an originating point of the world's own expression. Leibniz's concept of monads as persons forms the metaphysical background of Kant's concept of the autonomy and dignity of moral persons in the "kingdom of ends."

Now to reformulate this in my own way, the human-historical world exhibits a structure wherein each consciously active individual, or act of consciousness, has a contradictory identity as a self-determination of the absolute present. The world forms itself having such dynamically expressive monads as centers. It realizes its own order therein. We express the world as the world's individual acts; and each individual act has its own unique position as a self-forming individual. I hold that the world's moral order is grounded in this existential fact.

In this framework, the concept of the act as something merely passively determined, as in the model of physical causation appropriate to object logic, is entirely irrelevant. Each act is rather an originating vector of the absolute present which enfolds the eternal past and the eternal future within itself. But conversely, each act is a momentary self-determination of the self-transforming matrix of the absolute present. As such the act is a bottomlessly self-contradictory identity: it reflects the world in itself, and reflects itself in the world (the absolute other). Thus the act lives to die and dies to live. Each moment of time both arises and perishes in eternity. Or rather, each passing moment is the eternal.

I am fond of referring to Nicolas of Cusa's symbolism to represent this self-transforming matrix of the absolute present. There is, as it were, the infinite circle of God, the eternal present. Now because this infinite sphere has no circumference, every point, every act of consciousness, is a center radiating in infinity. I take this concept to be at the heart of Leibniz's world of the coincidence of freedom and necessity. Kant's moral imperative ultimately presupposes this existential fact, and yet it cannot, I maintain, be rendered intelligible in the merely immanentistic terms of Kant's own definitions of transcendental subjectivity. That is also why I have argued, in my essay on "The Physical World," that the physical world is already an aspect of the human-historical world with its structure of absolutely contradictory identity.

Kant establishes the transcendental forms of the understanding as the necessary conditions of cognition. But content without form is blind, and form without content is empty. He sees objective cognition as constituted in the synthesis of the categories of the understanding and the content of sensuous intuition. This gives rise to many problems, but at least Kant thought there is a thing-in-itself outside transcendental subjectivity. In the Neo-Kantian school, however, they say that to understand Kant is to transcend Kant, and they do so by proclaiming the primacy of the moral domain over the domain of cognition. They say that existence *(Sein)* does not yield the moral ought *(Sollen)*. And *Sein* is something essentially conceived of by applying the forms of judgment; it is so-called objective existence. Needless to say, the thinking subject itself cannot properly be clarified from the standpoint of objective existence.

How then is the thinking subject to be articulated? Is it a not-being? How can it be said that a nonentity thinks, or that a not-being acts? We might try to say that the self exists but is inconceivable. But how can we even conceive of the inconceivable? When we do so, is it not already thought? To say that the self is inconceivable would seem to mean that it cannot become an object to itself. This is exactly the case. And yet the self cannot be clarified with a merely negative definition.

How to proceed positively? We can say that the self exists at the point where that which cannot become an object in one dimension becomes an object in another dimension—perhaps in some higher dimension. But even conceiving of an infinitely higher objective dimension will not give us sufficient grounds on which to clarify what the self is. I say there has to be an absolute about-face from this objective approach. In my view, the self can only be grasped as a form of contradictory identity, in the transpositional logic I have indicated above.

Now what in general is the logical meaning of the proposition that a thing exists? Aristotle has one definition. He says that that which is grammatical subject and cannot become predicate —that is, the individual substance—is what is truly real. Leibniz expands on this definition by maintaining that a "complete substance" contains an infinite number of predicates, all of which are essential to it. In my logic of dynamic expression, neither definition adequately clarifies the thinking, active self. Neither Aristotle's _entelekeia_ nor ever Leibniz's self-causing monad accounts for how the self must first become its own predicate—something which predicates of itself by negating itself—and thus becomes self-expressive and self-conscious. Something merely teleological is not yet self-reflective; nor is it self-conscious in the full sense I have indicated. It is still, to my way of thinking, something objectified.

That which is self-conscious must stand, self-consciously, in a dynamically expressive relation to an absolute other. This entails the biconditional structure of co-origination and co-reflection. Thus I repeat that I disagree altogether with the epistemological position that takes its point of departure from the logic of objects. I hold that thinking takes place within the structure of an interexpressive relation. Judgment itself occurs within the contradictory identity of subject and object. From A, A expresses B in itself, as something expressed by A. That is, taking B as grammatical subject, A predicates of B; alternatively, taking B as object, A predicates of B. But the converse is also true. It can equally be said that A is expressed in B, becomes a perspective of B's own expression.

To bring out this logic of contradictory identity in respect to human consciousness I have often used the formula _we think by becoming things_, and _we act by becoming things_. When that which opposes the self is conceived of as a form of merely spatial opposition, the self is reduced to being an objective thing too. This kind of spatial opposition is appropriate to the framework of object logic, which accounts for the mere action and reaction of objective things. But unfortunately, thinkers often conceive of knowing merely as a variety of interaction in this sense. Even the initial formulations of Kant's *Kritik der reine Vernunft* do not entirely escape this dogmatism. And yet cognition has no meaning from such a perspective. A conscious act has to be understood as a form of dynamic, reciprocal expression; and this takes place in the structure of contradictory identity I have articulated above. In this framework, what Leibniz calls activity and passivity—in contrast to the mere action and reaction of objects—constitute contradictory poles of a transpositional matrix. A conscious act can then be understood as a transformative function of the matrix itself, which has this structure of contradictory identity. This is also the reason physical phenomena can be understood as the transformations of an energy field.

Each center of the matrix's self-transformation is what I call a self-determination of the matrix through the contradictory identity of the many and the one—of that which changes and that which is changed. It is in this kind of transformational matrix that the self negates itself, and thereby expresses itself. The act is individual precisely through its self-negation (and thereby its self-expression). Subject and object in expression—or again, the I-Thou relation—has this form of dynamic reciprocity. Even if consciousness is not a factor, we are actually considering it from the standpoint of self-consciousness—the standpoint of one who is self-expressive in the full monadological sense. Such a standpoint is the *sine qua non*. This unifying transpositional matrix is always required to define the form of dynamic expression.

The direction of infinite self-determination, in which the matrix transforms itself in itself, is liable to be understood, Spinozistically, as an objective one. Object logic wants to see conscious reality, the world of interactive monads, from such a perspective. Aristotle's concept of the grammatical subject already represents the logic of objective predication as far as it can go. I say, however, that something objectively determined is itself to be rendered as a self-determination of a mediating universal; and accordingly, a subject of predication has to be understood as the self-determination of a predicative universal (as in Kant's transcendental epistemology).

Now in Aristotle's framework, the world is predicated as an attribute of a self-identical unity, or grammatical subject; that is why the predicates become the activities of objectively real units, or substances. I contend, however, that conscious expression has no meaning in these terms. It can only begin to take on meaning in the framework of a self-determining noetic field (in Kant's sense). The being of the grammatical subject presupposes this kind of transcendental being of the predicate. (Plato's "essences" would seem to pertain to this latter assumption.) Self-conscious being pertains to noetic self-determination in this sense. Our conscious being has meaning in this framework. Each conscious act appears as a self-contradictory center of the noetic field of predicates. Reflection is nothing other than the self-reflection of the noetic field within itself. Our conscious acts are grounded in such a standpoint. That is the basis on which we are self-conscious and moral.

From the standpoint of this "logic of the predicate" the conscious world expresses itself within itself. It forms itself by expressing itself. The biological world already begins to exhibit this structure in its movement from the formed to the forming, as a system of the contradictory identity of its temporal and spatial functions. That is why activity as the mutual transaction among individuals, or organisms, in the biological world is always teleological. Units of biological life do not merely oppose one another; they intervolve one another symbiotically. Here for the first time, in contrast to the physical world, active beings are describable in dynamically formative terms.

But I have said that the biological world is still partially spatial and material. It is not fully coextensive with the human-historical world, which is structured as an identity of absolute contradiction. In the world of true concrete actuality—the human-historical world that exists and moves through itself as its own transformational matrix—time is always the negation of space, just as space is the negation of time. In this transpositional form the historical world moves dynamically from the created to the creating. The conscious act is creative without an underlying substance or ground, as the absolutely contradictory identity of space and time, of the one and the many, of object and subject.

The concrete historical world thus transforms itself in a

dialectic of self-affirmation through true self-expression (that is, through self-negation). Therefore it is always temporal, and efficacious, in the vector of its own self-formation. Conversely, it is always spatial in its vector of self-expression through self-negation. And it is Ideal in that its forms form themselves in the eternal present. In the latter respect, the historical world can be further determined as law. A law is an abstract form (universal) which determines itself as a contradictory identity of the many and the one. The historical world, in its temporality, consists of efficacious events as the negation of Plato's Ideas; and in its spatiality, of Plato's Ideas as the negation of efficacious events. It moves within a structure of dynamic reciprocity—from matter to form and from form to matter. The world's monads are interactive, in this transpositional sense, in the matrix of the eternal present. Each existential monad originates itself by expressing itself; and yet it expresses itself by negating itself and expressing the world. The monads are thus co-originating, and form the world through their mutual negation. The monads are the world's own perspectives; they form the world interexpressively through their own mutual negation and affirmation. Conversely, the concrete matrix of historical actuality that exists and moves through itself enfolds these monadic perspectives within itself. It transforms itself by having the monads as its centers.

It is in the historical world-time of the absolute present that the monads form the individual expressions of the world. They are both self-originating and co-originating in the matrix of the absolute present. Our own activities as microcosms of the world may be thought to constitute unique events in world-time while simultaneously representing the Ideas as the world's self-negation (that is, self-expression) in world-space. Our activities thereby acquire universality and value. Conversely, the Ideas, as the world's own expressions and values, entail a negation of negation: they are affirmative, actual, self-forming, and at the very least always have moral significance. That is why our activities in the historical world are always, and in various senses, both ideal and actual.

The self-conscious world of each individual human self is a self-determining monadic world; but as such, each self is a self-expression of the historical world. Therefore each self-conscious world is a momentary vector of historical world-space, which mediates its own objective self-determination within itself, and infinitely determines itself through its own process of self-expression. From the standpoint of the act of judgment, the world of the conscious self is to be understood as the noetic being of the transcendental predicate that includes the self-determination of the grammatical subject. Hence, in contrast to Aristotle's subject that cannot be predicate, the conscious self has its being as predicate that cannot be subject. The conscious self in the *Ich denke*, which Kant tells us always accompanies the presentations of the ego, would seem to correspond to this latter definition. As I have said in an essay on Descartes' philosophy, I think I can grasp the true meaning of Kant's contribution to philosophy from the perspective of my logic of the predicate.

Now conscious acts may be regarded merely as the mutual determination of beings that oppose one another. But this still does not account for the difference between material and mental. The latter, which has the structure of conscious activity, entails the interrelation between an individual and a whole. (I find that Lotze's metaphysics well clarifies this point.) A conscious act is a dynamic expression. It is a self-determination of a concrete transpositional matrix, a structure of mutual revealment of self and world. Our selves, the expressive monads of the world, constitute points of the world's own expression in and through our self-expression.

All life arises from the fact that it transforms itself by containing its own self-expression within itself. It is first biological and instinctive in a spatially predominant way—that is, it possesses itself as a form of self-negation. It becomes historical life as it becomes concrete in a temporal dimension—as a self-affirming form within a transforming matrix. In historical life there is always this dialectic of affirmative and negative: the former is the material world, the latter the world of consciousness, in the transpositional structure of the contradictory identity of matter and form. In terms of the logic of judgment, the former is the aspect of the grammatical subject, the latter the aspect of the predicate. In the terms of object logic, the former is the world of objects, the latter the world of noetic acts. Psychology, too, considers the world of consciousness to be a world of pure mental acts (for example, Wundt, *Grundriss*). In my essay "Life" I articulate the world of consciousness, which phenomenology defines in terms of intentionality, as the self-determination of the temporal dimension of the world, having this transformative structure of the identity of contradiction.

Life-structures that contain the perspectives of the world within themselves, as structures of the world's own expression, may be regarded as instinctual in the predominantly spatial sense, but as conscious acts in their temporal character. Again, they are self-conscious structures in that they are co-originating expressions of the world. The world of freedom arises from this standpoint. The will arises as a dynamic perspective of the world. Reason itself is nothing other than a self-determination of the temporal dimension that always has the character of being a predicate that cannot be subject. We are rational in the self-determining predicate, or universal. Reason functions intentionally, as something temporally, consciously, and immanently enfolding the grammatical subject—that is, the object—and as having its own self-immanent *telos*.

This world of reason's own self-determination becomes the moral realm in Kant's domain of practical reason. Therein the grammatical subject, considered as merely self-expressive and as something expressed through symbols, is a world of abstract forms which, as forms, exhibit the structure of the contradictory identity of the many and the one—that is, a world of pure law. Our selves, as individuals that merely express the world, as mere thinking beings, express the world formally. But as these formal worlds we also form ourselves—that is, we are pure wills. This is the moral will, whose purpose lies in respecting the law, obeying the moral law for its own sake, and always living in accord with duty. Moral duty becomes a categorical imperative for the rational self. Recognition of the person of the other—involving, I might add, the structure of the contradictory identity of persons and their mutual determination in the form of the contradictory identity of the many and the one—is precisely the way the self becomes a moral person. The other person becomes a moral person in the same way.

Kant therefore says that we must treat a person always as an end in himself/herself and never as a means, both in the case of our own person and that of another person. This moral world is Kant's "kingdom of ends." When we conceive of the world of objective moral behavior from the perspective of the mere conscious self, however, we only get a world of pure ego and merely formal will. Kant's philosophy is limited to the transcendental standpoint. When such a world of pure transcendental ego is conceived of in reference to the grammatical subject—that is, spatially, as an order of coexistence—it becomes the world of "pure cognition." Kant's "consciousness in general" is formulated from such a standpoint.

Kant emphasizes sensuous intuition even more than the Neo-Kantian school. He conceives of the phenomenal world in terms of sensuous intuition, formed through the categories of the understanding in the act of judgment. The opposing view to Kant's definition of the phenomenal world as the determination of the predicate is to regard it as determined from its own standpoint. This latter standpoint, that of the grammatical subject, becomes a necessary world—what Kant calls the world of nature.

In my view, the phenomenal world is spatial in the form 'from many to one' (the one negating the many), and yet is temporal in the form 'from one to many' (the many negating the one). This is the self-contradictory structure of the conscious act. The natural world is schematized, to use Kant's word, by having these transforming perspectives as centers. The self-origination of these centers may be regarded as the acts of imagination in the dimension of consciousness; in the dimension of practical reason, the schemata are laws that appear as self-determinations of the predicate. From my standpoint, the *Ding-an-sich* is nothing other than the transforming matrix in which the self finds itself—the matrix of the self-forming historical world that is immediately expressed in the self. Accordingly, I think I can subsume Kant's philosophy within my own logic of the human-historical world.

I will append here a final word about my logic of the predicate. The historical world, I say, is always self-expressive in the dynamically transformative structure of the conscious act as the contradictory identity of the many and the one. Its self-expression is its self-negation, and is, as it were, symbolic by exhibiting a predicative character. Thus in the world of symbolic self-expression, which is to say the world that determines itself in the form of judgment, the direction that is self-determining and self-affirming may be defined in the categories of the grammatical subject while the contrary direction that is an expression of self-negation may be defined in terms of the transcendental predicate.

Speaking from the side of the grammatical subject, the predicate becomes its attribute; the predicate is not something autonomous in itself, but can only be predicated in reference to the subject. In this frame of reference, the predicate is merely abstract or universal. But something that does not express itself in any sense would be a mere nonentity. Accordingly, a grammatical subject, or a particular thing, is a subject *of expression;* it has to be conceived through a logic of the predicative universal's own self-determination. My own transpositional logic conceives of these two opposing directions of subject and predicate as the self-determination of a "dialectical universal," which I also refer to as "the place of nothingness." Grammatical subject and predicate express the transcendent and immanent planes of this "place," our historical reality that transforms itself without underlying substance or ground. A substantive one or ground is to be found in neither plane, or direction.

The conscious world, having the form of a contradictory identity, expresses itself through self-negation and creates itself through self-affirmation. It has a spatial character in respect of the one negating the many in the order of coexistence, and is temporal in respect of the many negating the one in the order of occurrence. (Time and space are not independent forms, but only dimensions of the self-transforming matrix of space-time.) The conscious world transforms itself as a movement from the formed to the forming—it is self-forming in this way, through its own self-expression—and it transforms itself by way of this self-expression in the forms of its space-time vectors, as the contradictory identity of the many and the one.

From the standpoint of symbolic self-determination—that is, at the ultimate point of that form of self-negation in the theoretical consciousness by which the self-forming world determines, or expresses, itself through its own self-negation—the act of formation becomes the act of judgment. Therefore, from the perspective of the world's own self-formation—that is, from the standpoint of the concrete matrix that is self-determining through the act of judgment—subject and predicate are related as the aspects of object and noetic act, respectively. The objective element predominates in its movement from the *formed to the forming,* or from the *determined* to the determining, where we emphasize the aspect of a *definite* form, something *created.* Conversely, in the concrete matrix that takes form through an object's being present to a subject, everything is likewise to be understood as having the character of a predicate, or as the *self-determination* of the predicative universal through the act of judgment, and thus as something that *determines itself* on its own ground.

Therefore, to consider the grammatical subject from the side of the predicate is to regard the act of judgment as the self-determination of a predicative universal. It is to consider it in the framework of the noetic act by probing the depths of noesis itself. That the noetic act possesses itself as pure act signifies that the universal possesses itself in its own self-determination, and this, in turn, signifies that it has a temporal character. Therefore the universal is its own process of particularization, and, at its ultimate point, of its own individualization. But, at the same time, this has the inverse significance that the universal possesses itself through the negation of its individual determinations, and that it cannot be determined in the form of an individual as grammatical subject. It possesses itself by its own self-negation through which it negates the determination of the grammatical subject.

Probing the depths of noesis, the noetic act, as a determination having the structure of a contradictory identity of the many and the one, is spatial as the negation of the many, and yet is temporal as the affirmation of the many. An act of consciousness is thus spatial-temporal.

The world is self-forming through its own self-expression in the dialectic involving subject and object of expression. From the standpoint of the act of judgment in the form of the grammatical subject, it may finally be regarded as the world of Spinoza's substance—something that is absolutely determined as a spatial order of coexistence. In the form of the predicate, however, it may be regarded as Kant's world of transcendental logic, or a self-determination of a self-determining universal that has a temporal character. From this latter standpoint, the grammatical subject becomes an object for a subject, as the self-determination of the predicative plane. From this same standpoint, we can conceive rationally of the world as an identity of *Sollen* and *Sein*, and generate the moral imperative "you must act, therefore you can act."

Just as the self-determining universal, by possessing itself in self-negation (self-expression), becomes the grammatical subject, so too the world becomes a synthetic unity, a "consciousness in general," through the negation of the individual and the affirmation of the universal. (Hence, in the dynamically transformative structure of historical reality, both subjective and predicative dimensions possess themselves in self-negation, or interexpressively.) Form and matter are interrelated in this dialectic of negation and affirmation. That which is given is material and individual in the dimension of the grammatical subject; it is formal as a synthetic unity in the dimension of the predicate. The self-determinations of the predicative dimension function as categoreal determinations insofar as they function as the forms of cognitive construction.

From this standpoint, the act of judgment is a self-determination of the world that is symbolically self-expressive. Subject and predicate, object and mental act, are related in a structure of contradictory identity; and being can be conceived through the contradictory directions of these parameters. But I repeat that true reality, which exists and moves in and through itself, is to be found, one-sidedly, in neither direction. True reality is historical reality, and it consists in the dynamically contradictory identity of these parameters. Therefore, the being of the self is not merely theoretically transcendental. As a self-determination of the self-transforming historical world, it consists in the contradictory identity of object and subject in the transformation from the created to the creating. It exists by having an active, volitional character.

2

In the position I am articulating, the self is to be understood as existing in that dynamic dimension wherein each existential act of consciousness, as a self-expressive determination of the world, simultaneously reflects the world's self-expression within itself and forms itself through its own self-expression.

The self thus exists as the negation of the world's spatial dimension insofar as it is a self-determination of the temporal vector of the world which transforms itself through the contradictory identity of space and time. Or again, in Kant's framework of the transcendental grounds of judgment, the conscious self exists as the self-determination of the predicative plane insofar as it is formative of the plane of the grammatical subject, that is, of the world which expresses itself in the form of the contradictory identity of objectivity and subjectivity. The conscious self pertains to that self-determination of subjectivity which determines itself as objectivity. The individual act is nothing other than this existential place of dynamic expression. The dynamic world is always this contradictory identity of the spatial and temporal, objective and subjective, transcendent and immanent planes of the act.

By transposing these planes of determination, the self becomes a creature of infinite desires, at the bottom of which are the biological instincts. As functions of this kind of determined, biological universal, we act on the basis of hypothetical imperatives—that is, conditionally.

On the other hand, when the conscious self sees what pertains to the plane of the grammatical subject as its own self-determination, it sees objectivity as constituted by its own subjectivity. This constituting self is what is morally volitional and autonomous. It is something that reflects itself and possesses its own intentional *telos* within itself. It is rational as the self-determination of subjectivity itself. From this standpoint, we are active on the basis of the categorical imperative.

From the former standpoint, the self is a creature of physical desires; from the latter, it is moral. Indeed, the latter self is infinitely moral and partakes in absolute value as the self-determination of the dimension of pure time. In this way the moral self is a self-determination of the universal of practical reason that possesses itself, in respect of self-negation, as a one (rational universal) involving the self-negation of the many (sensuous desires). That is why the moral self has eternal life as its very *raison d'être*.

People who conceive of the religious form of life through the medium of moral perfection do so from such a standpoint. This is essentially what Kant's second *Kritik* amounts to. I will contend, however, that religion does not gain adequate definition from the moral standpoint. The religious form of life does not even arise from that standpoint. Even if such a thing were to be imagined, it would not be true religion.

True religious experience does not consist, as many people think, in an ethical progression from the finite to the infinite, from the relative to the absolute. It is first consciously realized when the self's very existence becomes problematic—when existence itself becomes problematic. The religious self pertains neither to the physical world that is the self-determination of the grammatical subject nor to the conscious world that is the self-determination of the transcendental predicate. Even though the self may first be discovered to be rational in the latter respect, the true self, the religious self, is not coextensive with the moral self. That is why religion transcends the framework of transcendental philosophy altogether.

From the standpoint of morality, the self's very existence

does not become problematic. No matter how evil the self experiences itself to be, it can become moral only on the presupposition of its own continued existence. To negate its own existence would be to negate the possibility of its own moral progress. Despite the fact that the standpoints of morality and religion must be clearly distinguished on this point, many people continue to confuse them.

When, then, does the question of religion genuinely arise for us? Where is the religious form of life to be located? I hold that the question of religion cannot be considered a question of value. Rather, it is only when a person becomes conscious of a profound existential contradiction in the depths of his own soul—when he becomes aware of the bottomless self-contradiction of his own self—that his own existence becomes religiously problematic. The sorrows of human life and its contradictions have been constant themes since ancient times. Many people do not ponder this. And yet it is when this fact of the sorrow of human life is reflected on at a profound level that the problem of religion arises. (Indeed, the problems of philosophy, in my view, arise from this same point.)

The self-contradictions of our desires do not have to wait for the words of the pessimist philosophers. We are always the pawns of our own desires. Is even morality, which is supposedly autonomous, really self-sufficient? The ultimate victory of moral good over moral evil would involve the negation of morality itself. The moral will possesses this self-contradiction within itself. It is perhaps for this reason that in Dante's *Divine Comedy* even the Greek philosophers are depicted as wandering about in limbo.

Now the fact of the fundamental sorrow and self-contradiction of human existence is to be returned, I think, to the existential sense that each person has of his own mortality. All living things must die. I too know that I will die in the biological sense. But my existential sense of my own mortality is something else.

In the biological sense I am still objectifying myself when I regard myself as a thing. That is merely the life of the flesh. Thus it is said that though we die to the flesh, we live in the spirit. To live in the spirit means to live rationally and morally, as the self-determining universal of practical reason. To live morally means then to transcend the biological: its *raison d'être* is eternal life, and biological death does not pertain to it. Hence for the moral reason to be self-conscious of its own death has no meaning, either. My sense of my own existential mortality, in short, requires another analysis. On the one hand, a biological thing must always, as an individual that lives in and through itself, negate the universal. An animal is essentially this, something non-rational. The human self is a consummate instance of individuality in this sense. But, as I have said, the human sense of dying does not emerge in such a framework. Nor does it emerge in the framework of the self-determining predicate, where the rational self can only be conceived of as existing, though not as dying, through itself. (See Descartes' concept of self-consciousness in this regard.) The requisite analysis, I believe, focuses upon another dimension of existence, namely, the self's own nothingness in the form of its own eternal death. In facing its own eternal death the finite self faces absolute infinity, the absolute other. It realizes its eternal death by facing absolute negation. And yet even this realization has the structure of an absolute contradiction. For to realize own's own death is simultaneously to realize the fundamental meaning of one's own existence. Only a being that knows its own eternal death truly knows its sheer individuality. Only a true individual, a true person, can achieve this realization of the inherent contradiction of self-existence. A deathless being is not temporally unique, and that which is not temporally unique is not an individual. The self truly realizes its own temporal uniqueness as it faces its own eternal negation. This existential awareness is not the same as mere noetic self-reflection.

In an essay on Descartes' philosophy I have already articulated the point that we achieve an existential awareness through self-negation in this radical sense. (Indeed, I have made it the point of departure of my philosophy.) When I realize my own eternal death, my eternal nothingness, I become truly self-conscious. I become aware that my very existence is an absolute contradiction. When I become aware of my own eternal nothingness I do not simply make a cognitive judgment. I am simultaneously aware of a deeper subjectivity behind judgment that in some sense transcends death and participates in eternal life. And yet if I were a being who merely transcended death I would not even be alive. Every living being must die—that is already a contradiction. My existence involves precisely this dilemma of immortality and mortality. What I have referred to above as the spiritual fact of religion is grounded in this same antinomy. It is not something that can be postulated from philosophy or morality. Rather, they too are grounded in it. It is the basic fact of our existence itself.

Death involves a relative being facing an absolute. For the self to face God is to die. When Isaiah saw God he cried out: "Woe to me! For I am undone; because I am a man of unclean lips; for my eyes have seen the King, the Lord of hosts" (Isaiah, 6, 5). What is relative cannot be said to stand up against an absolute. Conversely, an absolute that merely opposes the relative is not the true absolute; for in that case it would merely be relative, too.

When a relative being faces the true absolute it cannot exist. It must pass over into nothing. The living self relates to the divine, encounters the divine, only through dying—only in this paradoxical form. The framework of objective discourse will perhaps require us to say that when the self dies it cannot relate to God or anything else. I am not talking about dying in that framework. The absolute, of course, transcends the relative. And yet what merely transcends the relative would be nothing at all, mere nonentity. A God who does not create is an impotent God, is not God. Yet when related to that which is objective to it, it is not the absolute, but merely relative as well. And, if it merely transcended the relative, it still would not be absolute, either. This dilemma points to the self-contradiction in the absolute itself.

In what sense, then, is the absolute the true absolute? It is truly absolute by being opposed to nothing. It is absolute being only if it is opposed to absolutely nothing. Since there can be nothing at all that objectively opposes the absolute, the absolute must relate to itself as a form of self-contradiction. It must express itself by negating itself. Mere nonentity cannot stand in relation to itself. That which stands in relation to itself must negate itself. But by negating itself it is paradoxically one with itself. What is entirely unrelated to itself cannot even be said to negate itself.

In formal logic, insofar as things participate in the same generic class they can contrast with one another and be contradictories. But in respect of the absolute, if there were something outside it, negating and opposing it, it would not be the absolute. The absolute must rather possess absolute self-negation within itself. In this respect the absolute must be absolutely nothing. Except in the case of absolute being possessing its own absolute nothingness, that which negates it would stand over against it and the absolute would not possess its own absolute negation within itself. Therefore I say the fact that the absolute opposes itself as a self-contradiction signifies that nothing opposes itself. The true absolute must be an identity of absolute contradiction in this sense.

I hold that when we express God, or the absolute, in logical terms we must speak in this way. Because God, or the absolute, stands to itself in the form of a contradictory identity—namely as its own absolute self-negation, or as possessing absolute self-negation within itself—it exists and expresses itself through itself. Because it is absolute nothingness, it is absolute being. It is because of this coincidence of absolute nothingness and absolute being that we can speak of the divine omniscience and omnipotence. Therefore I will say that because there is Buddha, there are sentient beings, and because there are sentient beings, there is Buddha. Or in Christian terms, because there is God the creator, there is the world of creatures, and because there is the world of creatures, there is God the creator.

Speaking of God, or the absolute, in terms of negation in this way, I may seem to have returned to such thinkers as Barth, who holds that God is absolutely transcendent; though from another perspective of Christianity, this might be called pantheism. But these would be misunderstandings based on conceiving of the divine in terms of object logic. As I have often written, the absolute is not merely non-relative. For it contains absolute negation within itself. Therefore the relative which stands in relation to the absolute is not merely a part of the absolute or a lesser version of it. If it were, the absolute would indeed be non-relative but it would no longer be the absolute, either. A true absolute must possess itself through self-negation. The true absolute exists in that it returns to itself in the form of the relative. The true absolute One expresses itself in the form of the infinite many. God exists in this world through self-negation. In this sense, God is always immanent. Hence the old phrase that God is "nowhere and yet everywhere in this world."

Buddhism expresses this paradox through the dialectic of "is" and "is not" *(soku hi)*. I am indebted to Suzuki Daisetsu for showing me the following passage in the *Diamond Sutra:*

> Because all dharmas are not all dharmas,
> Therefore they are called all dharmas.
> Because there is no Buddha, there is Buddha;
> Because there are no sentient beings, there are sentient beings.

Another expression of this can be found in the saying of the Zen master Myōchō (Daitō Kokushi):

> Buddha and I, distinct through a billion kalpas of time,
> Yet not separate for one instant;
> Facing each other the whole day through,
> Yet not facing each other for an instant.

In these terms, a God merely transcendent and self-sufficient would not be a true God. God must always, in St. Paul's words, empty himself. That God is transcendent and at the same time immanent is the paradox of God. This is the true absolute.

If it is said that God creates the world out of love, then God's absolute love must be essential to the creative act as God's own absolute self-negation. The creation is not to be conceived of as an *opus ad extra.*

My idea here is not pantheistic. Perhaps you will call it panentheistic. But again, I am not thinking in terms of object logic. I am articulating the absolutely paradoxical fact of God as an identity of absolute contradiction. In my view, even Hegel's logic is constituted in the framework of object logic. This is the reason the left-wing Hegelians are able to understand his dialectic of higher synthesis in pantheistic terms. Contrary to this, I hold that the schools of *Prajnaparamita* thought can be truly said to have taken the paradox of God to its ultimate conclusion. Mahayana Buddhism's absolute dialectic is not pantheistic, as some Western scholars think.

The paradox of the absolute will be taken as a species of pantheistic mysticism by those who understand it from the standpoint of substance logic. To them I reply that this logic of the contradictory identity of the absolute is a "negative theology" in an entirely different framework. It is illustrated by Nāgārjuna's logic of the eightfold negation. Nāgārjuna's eightfold negation denies every possibility of objective predication—it is decidedly not a dialectic of substance that becomes subject in the Hegelian sense.

I will add that just as Spinoza's absolute substance can be called a *caput mortuum*, so too nothingness, mere negation, is not to be reified either. The true absolute possesses absolute negation within itself. It is by negating its own nothingness that it is infinitely self-affirming, infinitely creative, and is historical reality itself.

I have been developing this concept of the divine creation from the fifth volume of my *Philosophical Essays*. Creation does not mean that being arises from nonbeing. Creation in that sense would be merely accidental and arbitrary. Nor does it signify that being merely arises from being, either. Creation in that sense would merely be a necessary result, a form of causal determinism. Creation, real creativity, entails that the world, the contradictory identity of the one and the many, express itself within itself; it is its own self-transforming process in the form of a movement from the created to the creating. A God who is Lord *(Dominus)* in the form of a transcendent substance would not be a creative God in this sense. A creative God must possess negation within himself in order to express himself. If not, God creates in a merely arbitrary fashion.

This concept of creativity as self-expression through self-negation also pertains to the concept of the person. Past philosophers tend to conceive of the person merely from the standpoint of the conscious, but abstract, individual. Freedom is then regarded as the activity of an autonomous self. But even speaking in this way, the self must act from a certain kind of nature. If it were entirely indeterminate, it could not act autonomously. It must have a nature in some sense. Freedom means to act from one's own nature, to follow one's own nature. Mere arbitrary behavior is not freedom.

What, then, is the nature of the personal self? Where do we identify its essence? If it is taken to be an objective substance, it becomes a creature of mere instinct. Our true self is not to be found there. Hence, as I have indicated above, the self is rather to be comprehended in the noetic direction where the plane of the transcendental predicate constitutes the grammatical subject within itself. To say this in reference to concrete life, the world's temporal vector includes its objective, spatial dimension within itself. And that which infinitely determines itself in this dynamically expressive form is the act of consciousness.

In terms of this logic of the predicate, the nature of the self is rational, as the self-determination of the predicate plane itself. The self's subjective autonomy is then definable by Kant's formula that it follows the moral law for its own sake. I say, however, that when conceived of in these merely formal terms, the self remains the self-determination of a merely abstract universal —the self of no person and yet the self of any person. A self that merely follows the maxim of duty for duty's sake does not possess any unique individuality or reality of its own. It would merely be abstract being. The conscious activity of such a formal will would have no concrete meaning, for from it nothing particular or individual could emerge.

I say, therefore, that there can be no real activity in merely transcendental terms. The moral imperative here amounts to something like thinking idealistically. There is no account of concrete decision, the form of real experience in which the conscious self negates itself, and already transcends itself. That is why I maintain that only when the self's act is seen as a vector of the creative historical world can it be real conscious activity.

From this creative historical standpoint, even to think consciously is a formative vector of the world. The practical self that concretely decides is not merely rational in the transcendental sense. It exists by being able *not* to follow the moral law for its own sake!

The volitional self, the personal self, always has a self-contradictory existence in this sense. It exists as a dynamic subjectivity, self-consciously determining itself within itself. If its rationality, however, is construed in merely formal terms, the volitional self loses its concretely decisional and active character. Our active will signifies that objectivity is dynamically expressed in subjectivity. The mere subject that is not predicate is only an objective thing. When it is regarded as determining itself though its own predicates—that is, when it is regarded as functioning consciously—it becomes an instinctive and desiring thing. In this determined form it is neither free nor volitional. The free and volitional self, as a formative subjectivity, always expresses the objective world within itself.

I maintain, therefore, that the personal self exists as a unique, self-determining individual in that form of creative expression which has the structure of a dynamic reciprocity of subject and predicate planes—in other words, as the contradictory identity of objectivity and subjectivity. Thus the personal self functions consciously, but it does not merely exist within consciousness. Nor does it, of course, merely exist outside consciousness, either. The personal self, which is both free and yet determined, subjective and objective, exists creatively by being the world's expression and yet expressing the world within itself, as the contradictory identity of the transcendent and immanent planes of the conscious act. The personal self is a creative vector of the existential world having the form of this dialectic of absolute negation and affirmation.

The dynamic world always expresses itself within itself through its own self-negation; at the same time, it forms itself within itself and becomes creative through its own self-affirmation (the negation of its own self-negation). Therefore the term "world" does not signify for me that which stands over against the self, as it is commonly understood. It signifies the concrete world that has the logical form of a self-transforming matrix. It is absolute only in this form. (In an essay on mathematics I have said that even a mathematical system exhibits the logical form of a self-transforming matrix.)

Now it is this dynamic world, having the form of self-affirmation through self-negation, that transforms itself by expressing itself within itself. The absolute's self-expression may be understood in religious language as God's revelation, its self-transformation as God's will. In this dialectic of self-negation and self-affirmation, the world of the absolute present always reflects itself within itself; it possesses its own dynamic centers within itself. It is a self-transforming matrix in and through its own dynamic centers of expression.

Herein I see a kind of trinitarian relationship, analogous to certain ideas in medieval Neo-Platonism. As an individual center of the world of the absolute present, each self is a unique monad that mirrors the Father, the absolute One. Conversely, each self is the *Verbum* of the Father, as the self-expression of the absolute One; and each self forms the creative world as a spirit vector of the world. In this way the personal self is grounded in the world's own trinitarian structure.

My concept of the creative world as a self-transforming matrix involves neither an emanationistic nor a merely generative, emergently evolutionary world. Nor again is it a world of intellectual intuition, as people say who misunderstand me. It is always the existential world of dynamic individual expression, moving from the created to the creating—the world of the personal self, and of absolutely individual will.

In this respect, moreover, the creative world is a world of absolute evil. This is grounded in the fact that the true absolute expresses itself through its own self-negation. The true absolute exists in the form of its own dialectic of negation and affirmation. This cannot mean that God merely faces a world outside himself —the so-called world of physical nature. The world of mere physical nature is an atheistic, a God-absent, world. The deistic position, which discovers the external traces of God's operation in nature's designs, doesn't improve very much on the atheistic view. The world as the absolute absence of God is the world of Satan, one that completely negates the transcendent God (God who is Lord). It is a rebellious world; or again, it is physical nature as the ultimate limit of the self-negation of a transcendent God.

But the physical world is only the ultimate objective parameter of the historical world taken in abstraction from subjectivity. Nor is the creative world the ultimate pole of the self-negation of a transcendent rational designer, as Deism holds. It is another paradox, but God as the true absolute must be Satan too. Only then can God be said to be truly omniscient and omnipotent. This is the God who as Jehovah required Abraham to sacrifice his only son, Isaac (see Kierkegaard's *Fear and Trembling*). This is the God who has required the negation of the person itself. A God who merely opposes, and struggles with, evil is a relative God, even if he conquers over evil. And a God who is only a transcendent supreme God is a mere abstraction.

The absolute God must include absolute negation within himself, and must be the God who descends into ultimate evil. The highest form must be one that transforms the lowest matter into itself. Absolute *agape* must reach even to the absolutely evil man.

This is again the paradox of God: God is hidden even within the heart of the absolutely evil man. A God who merely judges the good and the bad is not truly absolute. But this does not mean that God looks indifferently at good and evil. To conceive of God as a supremely indifferent perfection does not square with the testimony of our spirit. This would again be conceiving of God in terms of object logic and by abstract inference. The existential testimony of our spirit may perhaps be dismissed as being merely subjective, but it at least squares with this account of the true absolute as having the character of affirmation through negation. A true logic must adequately exhibit the self-expression of the absolute. Therefore it must be paradoxical. True facts which bear existential testimony of themselves are always paradoxical.

Thus my concept of God is not entirely isomorphic with the Western medieval notion of a *Gottheit*. God is the identity of absolute contradiction that includes absolute negation within itself. This is well expressed in the *Prajnaparamita Sutra* literature's dialectic of "is" and "is not." If understood in terms of object, or substance, logic, the paradoxical structure of the *soku hi* runs afoul of the principle of identity. But for one who has personal experience, the paradox of God is a clear existential fact. The trouble would seem to lie, then, with abstractly logical thinking.

God is absolute precisely in the structure of the dynamic equilibrium of "is" and "is not." And the human self, God's own image, is similarly a contradictory identity of good and evil. Thus Dmitri Karamazov declares that the beautiful lies hidden within Sodom, and that the beautiful is both terrible and mystical: there is a battle between God and Satan, and the battlefield is the human heart.

Our hearts are essentially this battlefield between God and Satan. And yet the self's existential being as a volitional person lies herein. The self is always rational as the self-determining predicate; at the same time, it exists in that form of objective being which negates the predicate. So it possesses its existence in radical evil, in radical self-contradiction. From the moral standpoint, Kant refers to this as an innate propensity to evil. In my essay "Life" I use the word disposition in a similar sense. We have this disposition toward evil as a result of our bottomlessly contradictory existence.

This is another aspect of Cusanus' infinite sphere of God in which, because there is no circumference, every point is the center. The world of the absolute present is a bottomlessly contradictory sphere that reflects itself within itself. In this infinite mandala, as it were, the centripetal direction is the transcendent God, wherein we discover the absolute subjectivity of the creative, historical world. Its centrifugal direction, the direction of objectivity, is Satan. The world of the absolute present is always to be understood as filled with the demonic. We, the centers of this bottomlessly contradictory world, are both satanic and divine. Hence my theology of the absolute present is neither theistic nor deistic—a theology neither of mere spirit nor of mere nature. It is the theology of the existential matrix of history itself.

It is in these terms that I would clarify the way the self is essentially religious, and what the religious form of life signifies. The question of religion lies not in what the self *should be* as a consciously active being, but in the question of what the self *is:* not in how the self should *act*, but in the self's very *is and is not.* The religious form of life has nothing to do with a mere gulf and opposition between a perfect God and an imperfect individual. Even if there were an infinite gulf between them, the religious consciousness is not describable as a merely teleological (that is, linear) relationship. That is why thinkers are wrong when they try to ground the religious exigency of the soul in the standpoint of the imperfect self that wanders astray. A stockbroker also errs, and may even deeply lament his mistakes. To err in a religious sense does not pertain to the self's own purposes, but to the question of the very existence of the self.

I argue, accordingly, that the religious mind does not emerge from the self's sense of its own powerlessness in regard to the moral good as objectively intended—no matter how acute that feeling is—as long as there lies at the bottom of it any vestige of self-confidence in one's own moral power. Similarly, the feeling of repentance, when spoken of from the moral standpoint, is to be distinguished from genuinely religious remorse. It is legitimate to grieve over one's own moral evil from the standpoint of moral self-power. There can even be a sense of shame, which is always in reference to another. (Moral shame is also felt before an objectified, ideal self, one's own moral conscience.) In authentically religious remorse, however, the self itself must be thrown out, abandoned altogether.

Moral sentiment is always constituted in reference to an ideal other, and to society. Religious repentance is something else: it must refer to the bottomless depths of one's own self. It must refer to God who is Father, or to Buddha who is Mother. It must be an abandoning of the self in its existential depths—a feeling of shame concerning the very existence of the self. Only in this existential experience of religious remorse does the self encounter what Rudolf Otto calls the numinous. Subjectively speaking, the encounter is a deep reflection upon the existential depths of the self itself; and as the Buddhists say, it means to see our essential nature, to see the true self. In Buddhism, this seeing means, not to see Buddha objectively outside, but to see into the bottomless depths of one's own soul. If we see God externally, it is merely magic.

Why is the self essentially religious, and why is it that in proportion to the self's deeply reflecting upon its own depths—in other words, in proportion to its becoming self-conscious—the religious exigency appears and the self becomes agitated by the religious question? As I have said above, it is because the self has an absolutely contradictory existence. It is because absolute self-contradiction is the very *raison d'être* of the self.

Every being is a changing, moving being, and no being is eternal. A living being lives to die. There is no life when there is no death. Here too it can be said that there is already a contradiction. But a biological being does not know of its own death and something that does not know of its own death does not possess a self. In it there is no self. To a being that has no self, death has no meaning. We can even say that there is no death for a merely biological being. For death entails that a self enter into eternal nothingness. It is because a self enters into eternal nothingness that it is historically irrepeatable, unique, and individual.

Now to know of one's own death is to transcend death; and yet a being that merely transcends death is not a living being. To know of one's own death is already to exist while being nothing. To exist while being absolutely nothing is the ultimate self-contradiction. Yet the true self-consciousness of the self exists therein. We know that by transcending our own behavior. Usually this knowledge is called self-consciousness; but if it were merely so, the self could again be said to have a universal and rational existence. In that case, the temporally unique and singular self loses its significance and loses true self-awareness, too. Hence I say that there must be the self-negation of the absolute at the very ground of the existence of our individual selves, our personal selves. The true absolute does not merely transcend its own relativity. It determines itself as an absolute identity of negation and affirmation by including self-negation within itself and by being in relation to the form of its own absolute self-negation.

The world of the self, the human world, is grounded in this paradox of the absolute. God's creation is God's absolute affirmation through his own absolute negation. Or, in Mahayana Buddhist terms, because there is Buddha there are sentient beings, and because there are sentient beings there is Buddha. The human self's relation to the absolute is not a matter of imperfection, but of the self-negation of the absolute. Hence I repeat Daitō Kokushi's verse to express the paradoxical identity of the human and the divine:

> Buddha and I, distinct through a billion kalpas of time,
> Yet not separate for one instant;
> Facing each other the whole day through,
> Yet not facing each other for an instant.

The relation between God and the human self is the paradox of the absolute, the simultaneous presence and absence of Buddha and Daitō. The religious consciousness does not arise out of our own selves; it is simultaneously the call of God or Buddha. It is the working, the operation, of God or Buddha welling up from the bottomless depths of the soul. St. Augustine cries out, at the beginning of his *Confessions*, "You have created us for you, O Lord, and our hearts will not rest until they rest in you." Some thinkers neglect this point and try to conceive of God and to discuss religion merely from the human side. They are not even aware of the clear distinction between religious and moral questions. This is comparable to shooting a bow while blindfolded.

Needless to say, morality is one of the highest human values. But religion does not necessarily take morality as its medium or its vehicle. In the religious relation between the self and the absolute, which is the very source of the life of the self, the wise man and the fool, the good man and the evil man, are all equal. As Saint Shinran has said: "If even the good man attains salvation, how much more so the evil man." In the human world, which is essentially self-contradictory, the opportunities which lead us to religion exist everywhere. Religion is the absolute overturning of values in this sense. And for the proud moralist to gain religious faith may indeed be said to be more difficult than for a camel to pass through the eye of a needle.

Christianity, which is personalistic, places the fountainhead of religion in man's fall in an extremely acute way. Original sin is transmitted to the descendants of Adam, who rebelled against God, the creator. Man is a sinner from birth. Therefore there is no way to escape sin from the side of man. The only escape is through the sacrifice of the son of God, who is sent into the world of man by God because of his love. We are saved by believing in the revelation of Christ. That man is a sinner from birth may be thought to be an extremely irrational idea as an ethical doctrine. But we cannot help saying that the idea of man's fallen nature as the essence of man is an extremely deep religious view of man. As I have already said, it must actually express a fundamental fact of human life. The human is established by the absolute self-negation of God; and in his very essence, man is fated to be thrown into the eternal flames of hell.

In the True Pure Land sect *(Jōdo Shinshū)* as well, man is seen as intrinsically sinful. It speaks of sentient beings who are "deeply wicked and possess fiery evil passions." It says that man is saved only by relying on Amida Buddha. In Buddhism, the essence of man is understood to exist in illusion. Illusion is the fountainhead of all evil. Illusion arises when we conceive of the objectified self as the true self. The source of illusion is in seeing the self in terms of object logic. It is for this reason that Mahayana Buddhism says that we are saved through enlightenment. But

this enlightenment is generally misconstrued. For it does not
mean to see anything objectively. Were it to mean seeing the Buddha objectively, the law of Buddha would be the law of Satan. It is
rather an ultimate seeing of the bottomless nothingness of the
self that is simultaneously a seeing of the fountainhead of sin and
evil. Dōgen thus says that "to study the way of Buddha is to study
the self, and to study the self is to forget the self." This is a point
of view which is completely opposite to that of seeing things
through object logic.

Essentially, then, there can be no religion of self-power. This
is indeed a contradictory concept. Buddhists themselves have
been mistaken about it. Although they advocate the concepts of
self-power and other-power respectively, the Zen sect and the
True Pure Land sect, as forms of Mahayana Buddhism, basically
hold the same position. The two schools are aiming at the same
ultimate truth. If we speak about the difficulty of gaining religious faith, the more difficult way would seem to exist in the way
of the "easy path." As Shinran himself has said, "there is an easy
path to the Pure Land, but none who take it." In any religion, it is
the effort of self-negation that is necessary. Anyone who has once
awakened to true religious consciousness must act as strenuously
as a man attempting to be cured of a fever.

But from what standpoint, in what direction, does one make
this effort? To place God or Buddha on an ideal ground that can
never be objectively attained, and then for the self to make its
own efforts through the dialectic of negation and affirmation, is
typical self-power. It is not the true religious act. It is decidedly
not "the overleaping way to salvation" of which Shinran spoke. It
is the very antithesis of his teaching.

3

I have indicated above the framework in which I think the
religious form of life, its fundamental ground, and its existential
nature come into focus. I say that the religious question is not a
question of scientific, objective cognition; but neither is it a question involving the ethical imperative of the moral self. What is
the self itself, and wherein is its existential nature to be located?
Such questions pertaining to the self's very existence, to its bot-

tomless existence, are the ones that bring the religious form of life into focus.

It is the religious consciousness itself that is the source of our struggle with the problem of religion. The self does not suffer over something that merely transcends it, something external to it. It suffers over that which concerns its very existence, its very life. The more deeply it reflects on its own life, the more it agonizes over the religious question.

Now the moral conscience transcends this whole dimension of existential awareness. We can say it transcends the self from within the self—to that extent the pangs of conscience can shake the self at a profound level. From the pangs of conscience there is no escape; this moral anguish is ineluctable too. The self itself, however, still remains in its own moral anguish. Moreover, insofar as the self is rational it will continue to suffer in conscience.

Moral reason can be thought to be autonomous in this way. The moral self exists as the rational form of practical subjectivity, in which the moral act itself functions as a self-determination of the predicate. But my point is that the concrete self is not a mere universal, or merely predicative in nature. It is always a unique individual—and its volitional character has to be returned to that. That is why I say the existential self is to be discovered in that dimension where the individual negates the universal—where the practical self can say no even to the moral law. To define the volitional self in a merely universal plane would be to negate its freedom, and to lose it. The concrete self would be reduced to something geometrical, Euclidean, in that framework.

And yet I say the self does not exist merely by negating the universal, the rational, either. To define the self as something merely irrational would be to reduce it to being an animal. The more we pursue the concrete self, the more we discover that it is a coincidence of incommensurable parts. The novels of Dostoievski treat such matters in an extremely profound way. What is it, he asks, that truly makes the self be the self? What is it that is truly autonomous in the self? We cannot help thinking of such questions in regard to the self's existential condition. Indeed, scientific cognition and moral practice have their ground here too. Real value must always be grounded in real existence.

It may perhaps be argued that it is useless to become involved in such questions. For, as persons, it suffices that we follow the dictates of the moral conscience. It may even be said that the very process of pointing a sword of doubt at the moral life is evil. But if this were so, the question of religion would never come into proper focus. A person is not compelled to be religious, of course. Yet to speak of religion in moral terms is to set up social existence as the basis of the self's own existential condition. Religion, however, is a matter of the self's very life and death: while it may be thought to have a social basis, the existence of society itself is, in my view, returnable to the question of the self's existential condition. Hence I say that religious value is not a merely social value. It arises in a direction opposite to that. The sacred arises in the direction of the transcendence of value in the usual sense. It is the value that is the negation of value.

Now something self-contradictory has no self-existence. Needless to say, then, it cannot be an object, a grammatical subject that is not predicate. But it also cannot be something rational, a Platonic Idea, a predicate that is not subject. The latter does not contain self-contradiction within itself. And yet the concrete self exists as a self-contradiction. As the self deepens its self-awareness, it discovers its own incommensurable parts—its objectivity and its subjectivity, its spatiality and its temporality. It finds its existence as such a coincidence of opposites. The more it realizes its own discrepant parameters, the more it becomes self-conscious.

We must try to get to the bottom of this paradoxical condition of self-existence. The self, we must say, possesses itself through its own self-negation. It has its existence in a bottomless self-negation that is inconceivable either in the direction of the grammatical subject or in the direction of the predicate. Its nothingness is grounded in the contradictory identity of the creative world, which is self-transforming through the dialectic of its own negation and affirmation. At the ground of the self, therefore, there must be that which, in its own absolute nothingness, is self-determining, and which, in its own absolute nothingness, is being. I believe this is the meaning of the ancient Buddhist saying, "Because there is No Place in which it abides, this Mind arises."

When I speak of the depths of the self I am again liable to be interpreted as referring to a grammatical subject, some real "substance" as the ground of the self. But when I say depths (or ground) I refer to a bottomlessly contradictory identity of existential life. This involves an entirely different logic—the logic of affirmation through absolute negation. If we conceive of the self in the direction of the grammatical subject, of objectivity, then existential subjectivity disappears, as in the case of Spinoza's concept of Substance. If we conceive of it in the opposite direction, that of the field of the predicate, it ultimately becomes an absolute Reason, as in the case of Fichte's development of Kant's philosophy. There too the real self disappears. In neither direction is there to be discovered that bottomless depth of the real self's existence, which is to say its self-contradictory existence.

The logic of the existential self requires us to say that in the self's own depths there must be the fact of the self's own self-negation as constitutive of itself. This logic neither nullifies the self nor merely signifies that the self *becomes* God or Buddha—or can even *approach* God or Buddha in the way that the absolute is often defined in object logic. It indicates rather that the self and the absolute are always related in the paradoxical form of simultaneous presence and absence, as cited in the verse of Daitō Kokushi above. This logic conceives of the religious form of life as constituted in the contradictory identity of the self and the absolute.

Various misconceptions concerning the relation between God and self arise in the framework of object logic. I do not reject object logic, but I hold that it must be seen as only an abstract moment within a more concrete logic. If not, then even if it is called a concrete logic, it is not truly so. Misconceptions creep in when that which is conceived of through object logic is assigned a dogmatically metaphysical status as a thing-in-itself. The misconceptions arise from reifying the concept. I adhere to Kant in this regard.

I will repeat, therefore, that our true self cannot be found, one-sidedly, either in the direction of the grammatical subject or in the direction of the transcendental predicate. The true self rather appears in that dimension in which it predicates of itself through the logic of the contradictory identity of objectivity and subjectivity. Something that is merely inactive is a nonentity, in my view. The self must always be understood as dynamic, as consciously active. But the active self's existence is to be found neither in what is merely spatial as physical matter, nor in what is merely nonspatial, or temporal—in the so-called mental, or mere noesis. The self is a dynamic spatial-temporal vector: it is creatively active as a self-determination of the absolute present. By transcending the merely transcendental forms of space and time, it exists in the paradox of its actively reflecting the world. This has the form of a contradictory identity, the dynamic equivalence of knowing and acting.

The existential self discovers the self-transforming matrix of history in its own bottomless depths. It discovers that it is born from history, is active in history, and dies to history.

In the depths of the conscious self, then, there is always that which transcends it. And yet that which transcends it is not something external to the self; rather, the conscious self takes its existence from it and is conceived from it. But again, it would be off the mark to think of it as something like unconsciousness, or instinct. To think of it in such terms reduces it to the framework of object logic. Consciousness always involves the fact that the self transcends itself, goes outside itself, and yet simultaneously that things become the self and determine it. The act of consciousness consists in this dynamic interpenetration of subjectivity and objectivity. Unconsciousness and instinct are already transactional structures in this sense. My concept of active intuition as a transformational vector is a formulation of this. It is the creative world that transcends the self in the depths of the self. The more the self becomes self-aware, the more it realizes this.

The true self acts from an inmost depth that is the place of the contradictory identity, the dynamic interpenetration, of its own immanent and transcendent planes of consciousness. Intuition always has this significance of dynamic, historical expression.

Now intuition becomes active precisely because it is mediated by its own negation. It is expression through negation—a structure that transcends the ordinary dialectic of judgment. The latter refers merely to something within the consciousness of the abstract self. That is why it is again off the mark to interpret my concept of active intuition as a kind of intellectual intuition, as if part of the framework of Kant's transcendental epistemology.

Nor does my concept of active intuition refer to something like a mere aesthetic intuition, a way of seeing by objectifying a pre-existent conscious self. Active intuition is a seeing contrary to this. It means to see things from a standpoint transcending that of the preconceived conscious self. This is the creative world in the very depths of the active self.

Anyone who will deeply reflect on the self-transcending structure of self-awareness must notice this. Suzuki Daisetsu calls this awareness spirituality. He writes that the volitional power of the spirit is grounded in this paradoxical form. I will add that while this structure of spirituality is the religious form of life, it is not some kind of mystical transcendence. Essentially, that people consider religion to be mystical—that interpretation —is itself in error. I hold that even scientific cognition is grounded in this structure of spirituality. Scientific knowledge cannot be grounded in the standpoint of the merely abstract conscious self. As I have said in another place, it rather derives from the standpoint of the embodied self's own self-awareness. And therefore, as a fundamental fact of human life, the religious form of life is not the exclusive possession of special individuals. The religious mind is present in everyone. One who does not notice this cannot be a philosopher.

Every person has this religious mind. But many do not realize it. And even of those who do, few gain religious faith. Now what is religious faith, and what does gaining it mean?

People often confuse religious faith with subjective belief. In the worst extreme, they even consider faith to be grounded in the subjective power of the will. I maintain, however, that religious faith pertains to something objective, some absolute fact of the self. But it has the paradoxical structure of what Suzuki Daisetsu calls spirituality, too. In the depths of the self there is that which transcends the self. And yet it is not something merely external to the self, something merely other than the self. This is the dimension of existential contradiction, about which we are always going astray. Religious faith involves precisely this dimension wherein the self discovers itself as a bottomlessly contradictory identity. Subjectively, this discovery takes the form of "realizing peace of mind," and objectively, of experiencing "salvation."

In my view, this "salvation" is salvation from the self's own bottomless depths understood externally from the direction of the grammatical subject, or else immanently from the direction of the transcendental predicate. It is salvation from the desiring self and from the rational self. The religious self, psychologically speaking, discovers that it exists as something that has neither a merely sensual nor a merely rationally volitional form. It discovers itself as the bottomlessly contradictory identity of these two directions.

For the existential self to gain religious faith, therefore, there must be an absolute overturning of the frames of reference of grammatical subject and predicate in which the self is usually understood. Religious "conversion" is this revolution in the personality base. It does not mean, as people often hold, some kind of going from one extreme to another. Indeed, it is not a teleological process. The self is neither angelic nor animal. It is, rather, a being that is intrinsically deluded. By a total overturning, the self discovers its religious nature in its own bottomlessly deluded depths. Again, this is not merely a conversion from one extreme to another in a linear, teleological sense. An authentically religious overturning is what Shinran calls "the overleaping way to salvation," a radical revolution of the personality base.

Here again, religion cannot even begin to be described in terms of object, or self-identical substance, logic. But this does not mean that religious conversion, or "deliverance," involves a separation from one's own conscious self which is always, in one plane of its being, desiring, and, in another plane, rational. Still less does it mean to become unconscious. On the contrary, at the moment of religious conversion the self becomes more clearly self-conscious. This spiritual transparency is not something apart from the plane of conscious judgment—that is, the discriminating self. Suzuki Daisetsu calls spirituality a "discrimination that transcends discrimination." I take this to mean that religious spirituality is a wisdom that does not identify the self discriminately. And one who considers it to be mere unconsciousness has no understanding at all of the religious form of life. Such an idea is based on deducing the religious consciousness from the standpoint of object logic.

In a previous section, I have said that we exist as the absolute affirmation through self-negation of God, and this is the true meaning of creation. The true absolute does not merely transcend the relative. If it did, it could not avoid being a mere negation of it and, on the contrary, would become relative, too. Hence I have argued that the true absolute must face its own absolute negation within itself. It must absolutely negate, and thereby express, itself within itself. This paradox is articulated in the dialectic of "is" and "is not" of the *Prajnaparamita Sutra* schools of thought. We exist through the mediation of God's own absolute self-negation. Or again, we exist as the ultimate limits of the self-negation of the absolute One—that is, as the infinite many. We are images of God as mirrors of the self-reflection of the absolute One, and yet we are beings of absolute self-will. This is what is entailed in saying that we exist through the self-negation of the absolute.

Now the self exists in that it knows of its own death. It knows that it is born to die eternally. It is often said that we die for the sake of living a greater life, that we "live by dying" in a teleological sense. I repeat, however, that one who dies enters into eternal nothingness. Once he dies, a person is eternally dead. The individual never returns. One person is not two. If a one is thought of as two, it was not a living one in the first place. It would be a life conceived of externally, a merely biological life. Or if not this, it would be conceiving of the self's personal life as something merely rational. Moralists often speak of the self in these terms. However, the life of moral reason does not at all pertain to the world of birth and death. Here, too, life is conceived of externally.

And yet something that is merely birth and death endlessly transmigrates through the rounds of birth and death. This is eternal death of an irreligious kind. My position is rather that eternal life is gained at the point where birth and death (samsara) and no-birth and no-death (nirvana) are realized as one. Samsara and nirvana, the self and the absolute God, are for me expressed in that verse of Daitō Kokushi which refers to the paradoxical relation of simultaneous presence and absence of the self and the absolute.

I say that the self's eternal life is to be conceived of in these precise terms. It is not the case that the self, by transcending life, passes over into another life where there is no further birth and death. From the very first, there is, in the Buddhist phrase, "neither birth nor extinction." Another such phrase has it, "The eternal is here and now." This is the reason Kanzan Egen says, "There is no birth and death in Kanzan Egen."

However, there is always samsara, endless transmigration, from the standpoint of the self as an objective existence. Here there is eternal delusion. Now when the self realizes its own bottomlessly contradictory identity, it discovers the possibility of object logic as one of its abstract moments. Delusion only arises if one becomes attached to objective determination, to taking what is conceived of by object logic as concrete reality. This can occur not only in religion but even in the case of scientific truth.

We know of our eternal death. This is our existential condition. At the same time, we already exist in eternal life. Religious faith entails that the self realize its own contradictory identity of eternal death and eternal life; that is what is involved in religious conversion. Since this is impossible from the standpoint of the objectified self, we must speak here rather of the power, the working of God: faith is the self-determination of the absolute itself. Faith is grace bestowed. It is God's own voice in the depths of the self. This is the reason I say that in the bottomless depths of the self there is that which transcends the self and from which the self is to be conceived. It is from the self's bottomlessly contradictory depths that it realizes that "birth as it is is no-birth," the contradictory identity of the samsaric world and the world of eternal life.

In another essay I have formulated the position that the living world expresses itself within itself as a self-determination of the absolute present. It moves from the created to the creating in the dynamic equilibrium of its spatial-temporal character. It transforms itself through its own dynamic expression. Our lives are the self-determination of the absolute present in this sense. We are biological in respect of the self-determination of time, that is, as we are expressively self-formative. At its ultimate point, life is always this: "The present is the eternal present." It is always the identity of alpha and omega, the self-determination of the absolute present itself.

I say, therefore, that the religious self is self-determining by transcending the here and the now, by expressing the world of the absolute present, the world of the eternal past and the eternal future, within itself. And thus it possesses eternal life. It lives by being at each instant birth and death and yet no-birth and no-death. This is again the paradox of God: the world of the absolute, through its own absolute self-negation and absolute nothingness, determines itself and expresses itself within itself. The world of the absolute present thus has the form: "Because there is No Place wherein it abides, this Mind arises."

I will refer once more to Cusanus' infinite sphere. In the infinite sphere of the absolute present, each point is the center. Each existential center radiates to infinity: this is precisely my own concept of the self-determination of the absolute present. Understood merely in terms of abstract logic, without grasping the paradoxical structure of the self's own spirituality, these words amount to no more than a meaningless contradiction. In a concrete logic, however, the true absolute does not destroy the relative. The world of the absolute is the dynamic equilibrium of the many and the one, a world constituted in the relation of simultaneous presence and absence. In the paradoxical logic of the *Prajnaparamita Sutra* tradition, because there is absolute nothing there is absolute being, and because there is absolute motion there is absolute rest. The self always finds its true existence in this absolute paradox of God, the One that is the many.

Within this framework I endorse the saying: "The present is the eternal present." This does not mean that our life transcends time in a merely abstract way. Each instant of time, which does not stop even for an instant, is the simultaneous presence and absence of the eternal present. Each instant is the paradox of samsara and nirvana.

In the religious form of life, to transcend oneself is to return to one's true self, to become one's true self. This is the meaning of the Buddhist saying, "Since No Mind is mind, each mind may be called Mind." It is in the same framework that we can grasp the meaning of another expression: "Mind in itself is Buddha, Buddha in itself is mind." To think of the objective identity of mind and Buddha would be to misconstrue the point. It would be to employ a Western logic of objective identification; the *sunyata* logic of the *Prajnaparamita Sutra* tradition is another logic altogether.

Even Buddhist scholars have in the past not always clarified the Mahayana logic. That the religious self returns to the abso-

lute by discovering its own bottomless depths does not mean that
it transcends its own historical actuality—it does not transcend
its own karma—but rather that it realizes the bottomless bottom
of its own karma. The self realizes its *historical individuality* as a
self-determination of the absolute present. It is in this sense that I
understand such a Zen saying as "When I penetrate to the
Dharma-body, there is nothing whatever—there is only myself,
Makabe Heishirō."

That is why the Zen master Nan-ch'üan teaches that "the
ordinary mind is the Way." The Zen master Lin-chi makes the
same point when he says, "The Buddha-dharma does not have a
special place to apply effort; it is only the ordinary and everyday
—relieving oneself, donning clothes, eating rice, lying down
when tired." It would be a great mistake to understand these
shrewd sayings as referring to a condition of detachment and
indifference. They refer, rather, to a condition of total actualization of self: "Each step I take, my life's blood pours out."

To cut through the illusions of the discriminating intelligence is not to opt for a mere non-discrimination. As the Zen
master Dōgen says, the self must *realize its own* true nothingness. I interpret this by his own words in the *Shōbō genzō:* "To
study the way of Buddha is to study the self, and to study the self
is to forget the self; to forget the self is to be enlightened by all
things." I say that discovery in the scientific domain exemplifies
the same point. I call this seeing *by becoming things* and hearing
by becoming things. What must be negated is the dogmatism of
the reified objective self.

What must be decisively repudiated is the attachment to the
self conceived of objectively. The more the self becomes religious, the more it must, in forgetting itself, exhaustively use reason and emotion. But it is the corruption of religion if it is imprisoned in any determinate form. Dogmas are like a knife that
severs our life's root. Luther, in his Preface to the Epistle to the
Romans, says that faith is the working of God, who acts within
us; and, as in the first chapter of John, we are newly made to live
by God, we kill the old Adam; with our mind, spirit, thought, and
all our powers, we become entirely other men, and we are accompanied by the Holy Spirit. Zen speaks of "seeing into one's own
nature and thus becoming the Buddha-nature." But this Zen

phrase must not be misunderstood. "Seeing" here does not mean to see anything externally as an object; nor does it mean to see an internal self through introspection. For the self cannot see itself, just as the eye cannot see itself. And yet this does not mean that we can see the Buddha-nature transcendentally, either. If it were seen in that way it would be a fantasy. The "seeing" of Zen signifies an absolute overturning of the self. Thus it has the same meaning as the gaining of religious faith.

There must be an overturning, a radical conversion of mind, in any religion. Without it there is no religion. I say, therefore, that religion can be philosophically grasped only by a logic of absolute affirmation through absolute negation. As the religious self returns to its own bottomless depths, it returns to the absolute and simultaneously discovers itself in its ordinary and everyday, and again in its rational, character. As a self-determination of the absolute present, it discovers its own eschatological character, as a historical individual.

"The present is the absolute present" signifies that the religious self, as a self-determination of the absolute present, is free by virtue of transcending the abstract causalities of the here and now conceived of in terms of the grammatical subject or predicate. Even scientific cognition, the self's abstract thinking, is grounded in this freedom. "The present is the absolute present" is the paradox of God; the self mirrors the absolute as an existential self-reflection of the absolute present. I thus hold that the relation between time and the eternal *logos* discussed in Tillich's *Kairos und Logos* must also be conceived of in these terms. Both science and morality have their basis in the religious form of life.

4

Pascal has written that while man is merely a reed, the weakest thing in nature, he is a thinking reed. A drop of poison is enough to kill him. And yet though the whole universe should crush him, since a man knows that he dies, he has a greater dignity than that which kills him. Thus the reason human life is noble coincides with the reason human life is pitiable.

The sorrow of human life, I say, lies precisely in this contradiction. Human life takes its being from the world that moves from the created to the creating in the dynamic vector of space-time. The human self is, in its bodily character, material and biological. And yet the human self is conscious: it has its being in the form of the *historical*-natural.

Biological life already begins from the world's expressing itself within itself and forming itself self-expressively as a dynamic transaction of the many and the one. Space and time are its two contradictory parameters. Thus a biological being is self-forming, by expressing the world of the absolute present in itself as an organic monad of the world. It lives as a self-formation of the historical world.

An animal acts instinctively, according to the *telos* of its organic nature. And in their higher forms, animals desire. Pleasure and pain appear in the animal world of desire. An animal has a soul. The ensouled animal always desires to become the whole. Were an animal to become the whole, however, it would no longer be an individual, and it would then cease to be itself. For an individual is individual only in its relativity to other individuals. An animal is always this contradiction. It always faces its own absolute negation. It is born to be negated. It can never satisfy its own desires. Perfect satisfaction would be the negation of desire. Satisfaction begets more desire. The animal oscillates, in pendulum-like manner, between desire and satisfaction, satisfaction and desire.

Thus the wisdom of the ages tells us that human life is one of suffering. It speaks of fleshly lusts and sorrows because the human self is expressed in the flesh, in an animal organism. A truly human individual, however, is more than animal. What is animal is something predominantly universal, physical; it has a predominantly spatial character. In our truly human, space-time character, we transcend the determined, caused world of the here and now as self-determinations of the absolute present itself. We form ourselves as self-expressive individuals of the self-expressive world. We are consciously self-expressive in our intellectual, volitional, and conceptual life. We know our own actions. And we are consciously active. This is the respect in which the human self is dynamically self-predicating, and actively rational. That is why the human world goes beyond the merely animal world of pleasure and pain. Human life exhibits a whole array of sentiments and passions—joy and sorrow, suffering and anxiety, worries and frustrations. So again, the reason for the human self's nobility coincides with the reason for its misery.

The human self as an individual is the self-negation of the absolute. But the more it is consciously self-forming through its own dynamic expression—that is, volitional and personal—the more it discovers its own absolute negation in its bottomlessly contradictory depths, and thus faces an absolute One—faces God as God's own mirror image and opposite. At the very root of our individuality we always face the absolute face of God, and stand in the dimension of decision between eternal life and death. It is in that radical dimension of existential decision that the religious question opens up for us.

Barth speaks of religious faith as an absolute decision. And yet, Barth says, faith involves not just man's decision, but something objective. Faith is a responding to the voice of God. Revelation is God's own gift to man. But faith is man's obedience to God's decision through man's own decision in response. (Karl Barth, *Credo*). If St. Paul says, "It is no longer I who live, but Christ who lives in me," it is likewise true that one gains religious faith by a total overturning of self. He who does so attains eternal life; he who does not is plunged eternally into the fires of hell. In these decisions the will of God and the will of man confront each other.

I say, therefore, that only a volitional, a consciously active individual person can be religious. A thinker who would discourse on religion must deeply ponder this point.

In any religion, insofar as it is a true religion, gaining religious faith must proceed from the well-sharpened edge of the consciously active, individual will. Religion does not proceed from mere emotion. One only gains religious faith by a total exertion of self. As in the parable of the white path between two rivers taught in the True Pure Land sect, one always has to choose between alternative courses. There cannot be anything like an aesthetic religion. Persons may confuse the two through the word intuition, but aesthetic and religious intuition point in opposite directions.

Similarly, it is a great mistake to consider Mahayana Buddhism to be a kind of pantheism, lacking a concept of radical religious individuality. If anything, Greek religion was predominantly aesthetic, and fell short of expressing a truly individualistic religious character. Although of the same Aryan stock as the people of India, the Greeks took the road not of religion but of philosophy. India, by contrast, developed in the religious direction. In Greece, there was no realization of the true individual. There is no such concept, for example, in Plato's philosophy; and even Aristotle's concept of the conscious individual falls short of emphasizing the individual's sheer volitional character. In India, of course, there was even less awareness of the individual. But granting that Indian philosophy minimizes the volitional individual to an even greater extent than does Greek philosophy, there is at least a true concept of the *negation* of the individual. So we have explored the paradox that the individual in fact achieves authentic self-consciousness through realizing its own negation. In Indian philosophy one finds an absolute negation of the individual will. India therefore developed a concept of the religious, and from a perspective that is diametrically opposed to that of the religion of Israel. Moreover, Indian culture has evolved as an opposite pole to modern European culture. And yet it may thereby be able to contribute to a global modern culture from its own vantage point.

As the self-determination of the absolute present, our human space-time world moves from the created to the creating. If we place the emphasis on the past tense, it is a world of infinite causality. But while we are individuals of the world of infinite causality, since by knowing it we transcend it, as Pascal says, we are more noble than the whole universe that crushes us. The reason we can speak in this way is that we are the self-negation of the absolute which expresses and determines itself as a contradictory identity. We are the many faces facing the absolute One in a dialectic of presence and absence.

Therefore we always encounter the absolute in our own self-negation, reflecting the paradox of God. It is meaningful to say that we enter into eternal life and are religious in the dynamic encounter, the birth-and-death and death-and-birth, of God and self.

The religious question, then, is always a question of the volitional self, of the consciously active individual. But this has

nothing to do with the usual conception of religion as giving one
peace of mind. Peace of mind is not a religious matter; it arises
from a standpoint opposite to that of the problematic of religion.
It does not even qualify as a moral question. The desiring self,
which lives by a calculus of pleasure and pain, is only a biological
being, and not yet a true individual. From such a perspective, I
cannot help agreeing with those who criticize religion as a kind of
narcotic.

The self always encounters the absolute as the paradox of
God himself—that is, as the self-negation of the absolute One.
And thus the more the self is a consciously active individual, the
more it faces God. It does so as an absolute individual. The self
faces the limit point of God, the absolute One, at the limit point
of its own being as a sheerly individual self-determination of the
historical world.

In this sense, each self faces God as a representative of mankind from its eternal past to its eternal future. Each self mirrors
the absolute present itself as its unique, existential determination. Precisely, therefore, is each self a radiant center of the infinite universe. Adapting Cusanus, we can thus conceive of innu-
merable centers of the infinite sphere of God in a radically
existential sense. When the absolute is conceived of as self-determining in the absolutely contradictory opposition of the many
and the one, the world of individuals becomes bottomlessly volitional as the self-determination of itself. In this paradoxical form,
the *one* is absolute *will*, and the *many* are countless individual
wills that oppose it.

In my view, the human, consciously active, volitional world
makes its appearance from the standpoint of the paradoxical logic
of the *Prajnaparamita Sutra* literature. Precisely in these terms do
I find the meaning of the phrase: "Having No Place wherein it
abides, this Mind arises." The Zen master Pao-chi of Pan-shan, a
disciple of Ma-tzu, is quoted as saying:

> It is like waving a sword in the air. It is not a question of striking
> anything. It does not leave any trace as it cleaves the air. Nor does
> the blade break off. If our mind is like this, each thought is freed
> from knowing through concepts or ideas. The whole mind is Bud-
> dha, and the whole Buddha is oneself. Oneself and Buddha are not
> two. This is the true enlightenment.

I say that just as cleaving the air leaves no trace and the blade remains intact, so too the whole mind is Buddha and the whole Buddha is oneself, in the form of the contradictory identity of the consciously active self and the world, of the volitional individual and the absolute. Pao-chi's words are liable to be understood pantheistically from the standpoint of object logic, but they don't make any sense in those terms. They only gain meaning in this logic of contradictory identity: the absolute Buddha and the individual person are one in the paradoxical biconditionality of the "is" and the "is not" of the *Prajnaparamita Sutra*. The true individual arises as a unique, momentary self-determination of the absolute present. As I have indicated above, I interpret "Having No Place wherein it abides, this Mind arises" in this light.

The personal will is established by the self-affirmation through self-negation of the absolute. This is why the individual, volitional self is something neither merely transcendent nor merely transcendental. It exists as a self-determination of that concrete place of the contradictory identity of objectivity and subjectivity. And therefore, just as the moment can be said to be eternal, so too do we, as unique, consciously active individuals, encounter the absolute as its inverse polarity, its mirror opposite, at each and every step of our lives.

I believe this sense of unique, consciously active individuality is expressed in Lin-chi's words: "In this mass of red flesh there abides the True Man of No Rank: he constantly exits and enters through your own face." By unique, consciously active individuality I also mean the ultimate point of the determination of the human—facing God as the personal representative of mankind. Shinran captures this sense of individuality when he says, "When I deeply reflect upon Amida's vow which he contemplated for five kalpas of time, I realize that it was for the sake of myself alone, Shinran." These texts exemplify my own sense of the religious individual.

I say, therefore, that while morality is universal, religion is individual. I agree with Kierkegaard's view that the moral knight and the knight of faith stand in contradictory dimensions. Agamemnon's sacrifice of Iphigenia has an entirely different sense from that of Abraham's sacrifice of Isaac, as Kierkegaard's *Furcht und Zittern* so well brings out. When Abraham took Isaac early in thc morning to Mount Moria, he encountered God as the unique individual Abraham, a sheer human being, the ultimate point of real humanity. God called out, "Abraham." And he answered, "Behold, I am here." And yet Abraham the individual stood before God as the representative of all mankind. God said, "I will bless you; and I will increase your sons and grandsons many times over, and from your descendants all the people of the earth shall receive my blessings; for you have honored my word."

In religion, to return to God through the self's transcendence of itself is not for the sake of individual peace of mind. In religion, mankind transcends itself. Mankind touches the reality of God's own creativity—God expresses himself, and simultaneously we confront God in his personal revelation to us. To gain religious faith, therefore, means that mankind obeys the will of God through its own decision. Faith means, not a subjective belief, but confronting the truth in which the historical world is grounded.

The fall of Adam who ate of the fruit of the tree of knowledge of good and evil, in disobedience to God, is nothing other than an expression of the existence of mankind as God's own negation. The paradox of God's own negation is also behind the phrase of *The Awakening of Faith in the Mahayana:* "A thought suddenly arises." Humankind is bottomlessly self-contradictory. The more that humankind is rational and volitional, the more is this true. Humankind is born in original sin. In moral philosophy, the concept that the sin of the father is passed down to the children is highly irrational; but for religion, our very existence lies therein. To transcend original sin would be to transcend our own kind. This is an impossibility for us. Thus it is said that we can only be saved by believing in the fact of Christ who is the revelation of God's love. Through faith in Christ we return to our own source.

St. Paul says that we die in Adam and live in Christ. In a similar vein, the True Pure Land sect teaches that this world is always the world of karma, the world of intrinsic delusion and endless rebirth. It teaches that the world can be saved only by the compassionate vow of Buddha—only by believing in the wonderful power contained in calling on the name of Buddha. Calling on the name of Buddha is nothing other than responding to the voice of the absolute. It is possible to go directly from this perspective to the teachings of Zen. At the ultimate point of such a perspective, "Birth-and-death is no-birth" (attributed to Pan-kuei). This logic of contradictory identity entails precisely that "the whole Buddha is nothing but oneself," and "Oneself and Buddha are not two" (Pao-chi's words, cited above). Calling on the name of Buddha is like Pao-chi's "waving a sword in the air." It is like "skimming a stone on the surface of a rapid stream; the surface ripples and the stream flows on" (attributed to Chao-chou).

The religious relation, I have maintained, consists in the contradictory identity of God and the self. On the one hand, there is that which transcends the self and yet establishes it in being— that is, what is transcendent and yet the fundamental ground of the self—and, on the other hand, there is the unique, sheerly individual, volitional self. Religion consists in this contradictory identity of transcendence and immanence. It cannot be conceived of in merely objective or in merely subjective terms. It must be grasped from the perspective of the creative historical world which exists as the self-determination of the absolute present.

Every historical epoch is religious in its ground. The historical world is always the contradictory identity of space and time. It moves from the created to the creating through its own self-expressive transformation. As the many individuals comprising the self-expressive historical world, we are created-and-creating transformative elements of the world's own self-expression.

In such a world, we can speak of there being two directions in the self's existential condition of facing the absolute. The self faces the absolute present as the self-determination of its spatiality and of its temporality. The historical world is usually understood one-sidedly as a world of spatial determination, an order of simultaneous coexistence. But this is merely the natural, physical world. It is not coextensive with the historical world. The historical world includes the consciously active humankind. To express this fact with an old concept of mine, I may say that the human-historical world is the world of the mutual determination of objectivity and subjectivity, of the contradictory identity of the transcendent and the transcendental. In these terms the historical world is a living world, a self-creative world, expressing itself within itself.

Now in such a world the humankind, by transcending itself

outwardly, in the order of the simultaneous coexistence of objects, encounters that which is expressive of it—namely, the absolute's own self-expression—as an objective transcendence. Christianity may be said to have brought this objective direction of *transcendent transcendence* to its ultimate conclusion. Yahweh was originally the God of the Israelites. But having been purified by the development of the Israelites, and especially by their historical suffering, the concept developed into a world-religion of the transcendent absolute. The prophets were thought to be the "mouths of God" who spoke the will of God. In the period when they lost their native land and became the slaves of the Babylonians, the concept of Yahweh was deepened immanently and elevated transcendently by Jeremiah and Ezechiel.

The history of Buddhism reflects an experience of transcendence that is the reverse of this. Buddhism has encountered the absolute by transcending the self inwardly, in the temporal direction—in the direction of the absolute's subjectivity. The special characteristic of Buddhism, I will argue below, lies in this *immanent transcendence.*

The self-conscious self, I will repeat here, is neither something merely instinctive, a grammatical subject, a mere self-determination of the world's spatiality; nor something merely rational, a field of transcendental predicates, a mere self-determination of the world's temporality. It is the contradictory identity of objectivity and subjectivity, of the particular and the universal, of space and time. It is historically formative and volitional, a dynamically expressive vector of the world. As its own uniquely individual and volitional self, in this paradoxical structure of inverse polarity and biconditionality, the self faces the absolute by transcending itself outwardly, and, simultaneously, faces the absolute by transcending itself inwardly.

It is in the direction of transcendent transcendence that the self, as the self-expression of the absolute, hears its commandments and must obey by negating itself. He who obeys lives, and he who disobeys is plunged into eternal fire. In the direction of immanent transcendence, conversely, the absolute embraces us. It pursues and embraces us even though we are disobedient and try to flee. It is infinite compassion. Here, too, we face the absolute in our sheer individuality, as volitional selves. For love is the paradoxical identity of persons who face each other as individual selves. It is absolute love that embraces that which opposes itself. Thus the self-contradictory volitional self encounters an absolute love, which establishes it in freedom through its own contradictory identity, in its own existential depths—in and through God's own self-negation. In God's own compassion we experience an absolute love embracing us. Ultimately, the personal self is not established from a mere opposition of wills. That is why, in every religion, God is love in some sense or other.

The absolute does not transcend the relative, and that which is opposed to the relative is not the true absolute. The true absolute, I have said, must negate itself even to the extent of being Satan. Therein lies the significance of the Mahayana concept of expedient means *(upaya)*. This must signify that the absolute sees itself even in the form of Satan. Herein also is to be found the weight of Shinran's teaching that "the evil man is the true cause of Amida's vow," out of which insight grew his religion of absolute love. The more there is religious individuality, as in Shinran's other saying that the compassionate vow of Amida "was for the sake of himself alone, Shinran," the more this must be said to be so. It is by negating itself that the absolute causes mankind to be mankind, and truly saves mankind. Even such things as the "expedient means," the miracles, of the religious figures should be understood in this light.

Thus it has been said that Buddha saves mankind even by descending to the level of Satan. In Christianity, too, we can find the meaning of this self-negation of God in the Incarnation of Christ. Again in Mahayana terms, this world may be said to be the world of the compassionate vow of Buddha, the world of the Buddha's expedient means. The Buddha saves mankind by appearing in various forms.

I have argued above that the self can recognize two contradictory directions of transcendence in its relation to the absolute. These are exemplified in the Christian and Buddhist religions, respectively. However, a merely abstract and one-sided moment of the dialectic would not be a true religion. A merely transcendently transcendent God is not the true God. God must be the God of love. Christianity, in fact, teaches that God has created the world out of love. And this entails the self-negation of the absolute—that *God is love*. From this fact that we are embraced by God's absolute love, conversely, our moral life wells forth from the depths of our own souls. People do not seem truly to understand love. It is nothing instinctive. Instinct is not love; it is selfish desire. True love must be an interexpressive relation between persons, between I and Thou. I say, therefore, that there must be God's absolute love in the depths of the absolute moral ought. If not, the moral ought degenerates into something merely legalistic.

Kierkegaard has already linked Christian love to the moral imperative. There must be pure love at the ground of Kant's kingdom of ends. The moral person is established only on that ground. When love is understood as something instinctive and impersonal, human existence is being conceived of from the standpoint of object logic, the logic of the grammatical subject of predication. Contrary to this, I think it is consistent with the Buddhist view to see the moral life of the self as grounded in the world of the Buddha's compassionate vow.

Now the world grounded in absolute love is not a world of mutual censure. It becomes a creative world through mutual love and respect, through the I and the Thou becoming one. In such a dimension every value can be conceived of from the creative standpoint, for creativity always arises from love. Without it there can be no real creativity. That is why Shinran insists that "for the practitioner the Nembutsu is not an action or a good . . . for it is entirely due to other-power and is free of self-power." His concept of the "effortless acceptance of the grace of Amida" entails this kind of creativity.

We act as creative elements of the creative world, as the self-determinations of the absolute present. In the language of Christianity, our activity is eschatological, in the sense that God's decision coincides with mankind's decision. This is no different from the Zen master Bu-nan telling us:

> While alive
> Be a dead man.
> Be thoroughly dead,
> And behave as you like:
> All will be well.

From such a standpoint, we are truly historically world-creative as the self-determinations of the absolute present.

Now the Buddhism that took its rise in Indian soil was very profound as religious truth, but it did not avoid being other-worldly. Even Mahayana Buddhism did not truly attain to the world-creatively real in the sense I have just indicated. I think that it was perhaps only in Japanese Buddhism that the absolute identity of negation and affirmation was realized, in the sense of the identity of the actual and the absolute that is peculiar to the Japanese spirit. Examples of this realization are found in such ideas of Shinran as "in calling on the name of Buddha non-reason is reason" and "effortless acceptance of the grace of Amida." But even in Japan, it has not been positively grasped. It has only been understood as an absolute passivity to Amida, or as some non-discriminatory wisdom in a merely irrational, mystical sense.

My view, to the contrary, is that a true absolute passivity gives rise to a true absolute dynamism. I also think that there is a "non-discriminating wisdom" in the sense of a dimension of knowing that transcends and yet incorporates the judgments of abstract consciousness and determines their validity in respect of the ultimate form of judgment—what I call active intuition. Active intuition is fundamental even for science. Science itself is grounded in the fact that we see *by becoming things* and hear *by becoming things*. Active intuition refers to that standpoint which Dōgen characterizes as achieving enlightenment "by all things advancing." This is also the experiential foundation on which we obey God's decisions through our own decisions as self-determinations of the absolute present.

This non-discriminating wisdom does not mean a mere absorption in what is external as grammatical subject, or objectivity. It means to obey that which transcends us and causes us to be what we are, and to do so in the volitional, or dynamic, form of the contradictory identity of objectivity and subjectivity. Active intuition is a transformative structure. An activity that is truly selfless is actively intuitive. Moral behavior is grounded in it, and that is why moral behavior is religious in its ground.

One who is still imprisoned in transcendental philosophy cannot understand this. A true religion of other-power is required, and this can only be grasped in a logic of self-expression through self-negation. I believe that the religion of other-power, based on Amida's vow of absolute compassion, is congenial with present-day scientific culture in this respect. And does not the spirit of modern times seek a religion of infinite compassion rather than that of the Lord of ten thousand hosts? It demands reflection in the spirit of Buddhist compassion. This is the spirit which says that the present world war must be for the sake of negating world wars, for the sake of eternal peace.

The relation between God and mankind, needless to say, is not one of power. Nor again is it teleological, as is often thought. It is a relation of interexpression. The absolute does not destroy the relative; it possesses itself and sees itself in its own absolute self-negation. That which stands in relation to the absolute as its self-negation must itself be self-expressive through its own self-negation. Thus the relation between God and mankind is always to be understood as dynamically interexpressive based on the principle of self-negation. This principle cannot be grasped in either mechanistic or teleological terms.

The principle of self-negation requires an articulation of the absolutely contradictory identity of that which forms itself expressively, that which is infinitely creative, and that which is created and creates, which is made and makes. The relation between creative and created is then the dynamic interface between that which is expressive (creative) and that which is expressed and which responds expressively (the created).

This is the absolutely contradictory identity, the mutual revealment, of self and other. I understand the other through my own conscious activity. My conscious activity originates neither from the outside nor from the inside: self and other are co-originating through mutual interexpression. Self and other interact in this way. It is neither the self becoming the other nor the other becoming the self; the other simultaneously creates the self as its own self-expression. The I and Thou relation between persons is just such an interexpressive relation.

This dimension of dynamic self-expression is the dimension of intertransformation, and thus of mutual expression. Let me put this in terms of the absolutely contradictory identity of the many and the one. The expressive horizon arises on the side of self-negation—the many are co-originating. And the transformative horizon arises on the side of self-affirmation—each individual originates as the one. There is no world of self-expression that is not transformative, and no world of transformation that is not self-expressive. In the world of historical transformation, expression is a force, a formative vector. It is not merely something like "meaning," as the phenomenologists and hermeneuticists are saying. These scholars abstract expression from its vectorial character. Phenomenological meaning is the content of the world conceived of non-transformationally—at the ultimate point of the self-negating direction of the world that is dynamically self-expressive.

In the world of historical transformation, there is neither mere objective facticity nor subjective act. Nor again is there mere meaning. Concrete being always transforms itself through its own self-expression. Our wills have this character in a clear sense. In the past, the will has been defined, abstractly, as a function of mere consciousness. But there is no volitional act that does not express the world in itself. Will refers to the conscious activity through which we, monads of the world's own transformation, form the world as the world's own self-expressions while expressing the world in ourselves. In the historical world, even symbols have this dynamic reference to reality. They have the power of transforming the historical world as the self-expressions of the world.

Now what the theologians call the Word of God must be grasped from such a perspective. The human world, the historical world, arises from the standpoint where the absolute sees itself within itself through its own self-negation. This is the basis of saying that God creates the world out of love. The relation between that which is self-expressive and that which is expressed and expressive must be grasped as a dynamic interexpression— that is, in the Word. The Word is the expressive medium between God and mankind. This cannot be put in either mechanistic or teleological terms, and it transcends the determinations of reason as well. God and self face each other because God, in his absolute identity and will, expresses himself as the creative Word. This is revelation. In the Jewish religion, the prophets stood in God's stead and spoke his will to the Israelites, saying "Thus speaks Jehovah of ten thousand hosts, the God of Israel." They were also called the mouths of God.

I have said that the historical world always has its task, and that each epoch has its own identity in that regard. A true historical task, in a specific epoch, has the character of being God's own Word. In the ancient world of the Jews, the Word was something transcendent: "The Word of Jehovah faces and speaks to us." But today, I think it must be something immanent. It must be an expression that wells up from the depths of the self-forming historical world. And yet it is not something that is merely immanent. As the self-determination of the absolute present, the historical world always has the form of the contradictory identity of immanence and transcendence. It is the task of the true philosopher to grasp his own epoch's historical task in this sense even while he is immersed in it.

The *Word of God* is expressed in Buddhism, as in the Pure Land school, by the *Name of Buddha*. We are saved by believing in the mysterious name of the Buddha. The dialectic of immanence and transcendence, of mankind and the absolute Buddha, is grounded in expression, in the Word. That which expresses the compassionate vow of the Buddha is nothing other than the Buddha's own name. The *Tannishō* says:

> In his inconceivable vow Amida realized the name which can easily be held and called upon, and promised that "I will come to welcome those who pronounce my name." Hence if believing that "one will be able to transcend life and death by the help of the mysterious power of the great compassion and the great vow of Amida," one thinks that "my pronouncing the name of Amida is also the design of Amida," then there is no selfishness at all. Therefore one can be born in the true Pure Land in accordance with his original vow. If one believes this inconceivable vow to be the very truth, the inconceivability of the name is embodied within it. Then the inconceivability of the vow and the name are one and the same.

The inverse polarity, the mutual revealment, of the absolute and mankind is grounded entirely in the absolute's own expression, in the Buddha's name. We can conceive of this in neither sensory nor rational terms. Reason remains something immanent, the human standpoint. It is not the way to respond to the absolute.

I have said above that the self faces the absolute at the limit point of its own individual will. God, too, faces the self in his absolute will. (There is always this inverse polarity.) The interaction of human and absolute wills is mediated in the Word (as a dialectic of contradictory identity). The Word of God is something rational, a *logos*. And yet what is transrational, and irrational, is also expressed by it. The will transcends reason—indeed, it can destroy it.

Now that which transcends and yet faces us must be something that expresses itself objectively. Art is objective expression in this sense, but it takes a sensory, not a volitional, form. Religious expression must be absolutely volitional. It involves an objectivity directed at our innermost person. The Buddha transcends us, and at the same time embraces us. The perfect expression of this is found in Shinran's words: "My pronouncing the name of Amida is also the design of Amida." This is also the key to understanding Shinran's "overleaping way to salvation." It is based on the mysterious power of the Buddha's own name.

For any religion, any true religion, when a person gains religious faith, or deliverance, there always appears a principle of the absurd, which expresses the absolutely contradictory identity of God and mankind. This principle is neither sensory nor rational. It must be the Word of God, the self-expression of the absolute. It is the creative Word itself. Thus in Christianity it is written: "In the beginning was the Word." Concerning Christ, it teaches: "The Word became flesh and dwelt amongst us." In Buddhism there is a structural similarity to this teaching in "the Buddha's name is precisely the Buddha."

It is not the case, therefore, that the creative, salvific, and revealing Word—the principle of the absurd—is merely transrational or irrational. As the self-expression of the absolute, it authenticates our true self, and it makes reason to be true reason. This is Shinran's meaning when he says that "in calling on the Buddha's name, non-reason is reason." In calling on the Buddha's name we do not lose our rational consciousness; we rather function on the basis of that nondiscriminating wisdom I have indicated above. Something creative functions as the contradictory identity of knowing and acting, as the self-determination of the absolute present.

Now I have also indicated that the Word of the biblical God possesses the meaning of judgment as the revelation of a transcendently transcendent and personal God, or as absolute Will. It says that we are justified by faith. In contrast to this, in calling on the Buddha's name we are saved and embraced by Buddha through the expression of his infinite Compassion. In Shinran's perfect expression of this, salvation is an "effortless acceptance of the grace of Amida." It is effortless, spontaneous living based on Amida's vow. This has little to do with the usual sense of living "naturally." Religious experience cannot be conceived of from the standpoint of object logic, or of "nature" in that determination. Religious experience signifies that we are always embraced by the vow of absolute compassion. Without this compassion, it becomes something selfish and arbitrary—or else merely a logical game.

Truth arises in the concrete dimension where we open our eyes and see the world and open our ears and hear the world. The experience of compassion is like that. It functions as the self-affirmation through self-negation of the absolute. Any true communication with another person takes place in this dimension of "no thought and no conception." Even scientific truth entails that we know the world as self-expressions of the self-expressive world, as self-determinations of the absolute present. That is why in science, too, we can speak of effortless acceptance of the grace of Amida. Nor is it the case that compassion negates the will. True willing rather arises from it. The self is neither merely transcendent nor merely transcendental. It exists as the place of the contradictory identity of objectivity and subjectivity. This is the basic reason why we are beings who can be compassionate to others and who can experience the compassion of others.

Compassion always signifies that opposites are one in the dynamic reciprocity of their own contradictory identity. The religious will arises as the self-determination of this dimension of sympathetic coalescence. The will is instinctive in the form of objectivity, and rational in the form of subjectivity; but it is historically transforming in this religious dimension of compassion. Sincerity is a form of selflessness, a pure response to the other. Perfect sincerity is grounded in infinite compassion. It is this kind of perfect sincerity that I would place at the foundation of "practical reason" as well. Kant's ethics of practical reason was only a bourgeois ethics. A historically transformative ethics, I say, is one that is based on the vow of compassion. If the concept of compassion has not been foundational for Western culture (as Suzuki Daisetsu maintains), then I think there is a basic difference between Eastern and Western cultures in this regard.

I will leave the consideration of Zen, which has deeply permeated Japanese culture, to persons of the Zen Way. I want here only to say a few words about popular misunderstandings of Zen. First of all, Zen has nothing to do with mysticism, as many think. *Kenshō*, seeing one's nature, means to penetrate to the roots of one's own self. The self exists as the absolute's own self-negation. We exists as the many through the self-negation of the One. Therefore the self has a radically self-contradictory existence. The very process of self-realization, in which the self knows itself, is self-contradictory. Hence we always possess ourselves in something that transcends ourselves in our own bottomless depths; we affirm ourselves through our own self-negation. *Kenshō* means to penetrate to the bottomlessly contradictory existence of one's own self. Zen's principle of the absurd must be grasped as this paradox.

A Zen *kōan* is only a means to make one grasp this paradox with one's whole existence:

> One day Shuzan, taking up a bamboo stick, said: "When you call this a bamboo stick, you are wrong; and when you don't, you are also wrong. What, then, do you call it?"

Zen's principle of the absurd is not merely irrational. It is comparable to Shinran's "taking non-reason as reason." It is a form of the contradictory identity of universal and particular, of knowing and acting. It has a structure no different from that of scientific cognition.

I will refer to my own concept of creativity—the movement from the created to the creating—from this standpoint. This is the standpoint of the self-determination of the historical world. And it is the extremely "ordinary and everyday" standpoint that Zen celebrates as the self-determination of the absolute present. Lin-chi teaches: "The Buddha-dharma has no special place to apply effort. It is only the ordinary and everyday; relieving oneself, donning clothes, eating rice, lying down when tired. The fool laughs at us, but the wise understand." These words, however, are liable to be misunderstood, if grasped from the standpoint of object logic. To Lin-chi, ordinary human experience is eschatological in character. Moreover, the phrase "Mind is Buddha, and Buddha is mind" is far from considering life subjectively. "Mind is not mind, therefore it is mind": this contradictory identity of mind and Buddha, of self and the absolute, must be understood in terms of the paradoxical logic of the *Prajnaparamita Sutra*, as I have indicated above.

The various misunderstandings of Zen are based on object logic. What has been called mysticism in Western philosophy since Plotinus is something extremely close to Zen, but I think that Western mysticism has not in essence transcended the standpoint of object logic. Indeed, the One of Plotinus stands at an opposite pole to the Zen experience of nothingness. Neo-Platonism did not in fact attain to a religious celebration of the ordinary and everyday as we find it in the Zen tradition.

It is not the case that because our minds exist, the world exists. It is not that we merely see the world *from the self*. The self is rather something seen *from this historical world*. In my essay "Life" I argue that the world of the conscious self is the self-determination of the historical world's *temporality*. Every subjectivistic interpretation, by taking its point of departure from an abstractly imagined, pre-existent conscious self, beclouds our vision.

5

Persons who have religious sentiment from any standpoint, and who truly gain religious faith, are few. However, it is not that religion is a special psychological condition of special people. Insofar as the self is a historical reality born from the historical world, acting in the historical world, and dying to the historical world, it is religious. We should speak in this way in respect of the existential ground of the self. It is not that the absolute, which exists and moves in itself, transcends the relative. What transcends the relative is not absolute. This historical world exists in its encounter with the true absolute which contains its own absolute expression through absolute self-negation within itself. The historical world is always the self-determination of the absolute present in the form of the contradictory identity of the many and the one. Our selves, existential monads of the world, mirror the world, and, at the same time, are the world's own creative expressions. The self exists in this paradox, reflecting the absolute's own self-affirmation through self-negation. Thus the self, mirroring the absolute, possesses itself in its own self-negation. It is in this respect that we are always religious.

For the same reason, each of our actions is historical, and *eschatologisch*, as the self-determination of the absolute present. It is here, again, that we can say we obey God's decisions through our own decisions. Truth is revelation. The truth is known as *kairos:* it is *timely* in the sense of being the determination of the absolute present. At the same time it is thereby eternal and universal, transcending particular times and places. Each moment is eternity. Tillich's paradoxical relation of *kairos* and *logos* can be articulated in this way. I agree that the difficulties concerning the relation between eternal and contingent truth are based on an abstract understanding of time. Truth must be timely—timeful—as the self-determination of the absolute present.

That each of our actions is *eschatologisch* as the self-determination of the absolute present is what, in my judgment, Lin-chi refers to variously as "the total act," "The Buddha-dharma has no special place to apply effort," and "The way of enlightenment is the ordinary and the everyday." The interpretation of the eschatological here is different from that of Christianity. It is discovered in the direction, not of the objectively transcendent, but of what I have called the immanently transcendent. In its own bottomlessly immanent depths the self never finds itself; it discovers the absolute. Transcending its own existence in its bottomless depths to the ultimate limit of its own individuality, the self comes face to face with the absolute One. It transcends everything—this historical world as the self-determination of the absolute present, and the past and the future. In that immanent horizon of religious transcendence we are absolutely free. It is that absolute freedom which Pao-chi of Pan-shan describes as "waving a sword in the air."

Now I think that the standpoint of freedom which Dostoievski sought has to be considered in this light. There is nothing at all that determines the self at the very ground of the self—nothing instinctive in the direction of the grammatical subject, nothing rational in the direction of the transcendental predicate.

The self is bottomless. There is only what Zen calls the common-place and conventional—"The way of enlightenment is the ordinary and the everyday." In another variation on this theme, Lin-chi says, "When there is complete self-mastery, everywhere one stands is the truth."

I contrast the notion of abstract personal freedom in Kant, representing an extreme of Western thought, with this concept of absolute freedom in Lin-chi, who speaks from the depths of the Zen perspective. In Lin-chi's concept, we are, everywhere, the self-expression of the absolute. This does not mean that we are Nietzsche's *Übermensch*, but rather that we are men of God, "servants of the Lord." Those who think in the categories of object logic will be prone to interpret me as meaning that the self loses its individuality in the absolute. But that the self transcends itself in its own immanent depths does not signify a loss of itself; it rather becomes a unique expression of the world's self-expression. It rather signifies that the self becomes truly individual, a real self.

In my view, true knowing and true moral practice arise in this horizon of true individuality. From it arises the world of man-kind as the ultimate point of the absolute's own negation—the paradox of God as the contradictory identity of the many and the one. Shinran captures the existential character of this sense of God when he says that the eternal vow of Amida was entirely for his own sake. The more the self is individual, the more there can be this existential realization. This is the basis of my saying that the self exists in a relation of inverse polarity with the absolute.

In this paradox of God—that is, our face-to-face relation with the absolute in a dialectic of mutual presence and absence—there is the Zen celebration of ordinary human experience. It is the dimension of absolute freedom, as the self-determination of the absolute present itself. It is in this dimension that each and every point becomes an Archimedean point, and an exemplification of Lin-chi's teaching that "everywhere one stands is the truth." The more one is an individual, the more one stands in the truth, in one's own absolute freedom. But as long as a person remains bound from the outside, as it were, in the determinations of bio-logical instinct, or again from the inside through his own rational determinations, he is not yet truly free in the religious sense.

This absolute religious freedom arises from a perspective

that is diametrically opposed to the prevailing concept of freedom in modern Western culture. The latter is an abstract freedom, something merely Euclidean. In the logical articulation of this absolute religious freedom I am also opposed to Western mystical philosophy in that the true individual must be established from the absolute's own existential negation. Those who consider my philosophy to be itself mystical are thinking from the standpoint of object logic.

Now in my logic, absolute negation functions to affirm the religious character of ordinary human experience, not to negate it. Even though it has not yet been developed theoretically, I think that the dynamic interresonance of absolute negation and our everyday life is exemplified in Japanese culture. Mutai Risaku has argued that the Japanese spirit appears equally in the poetry of the *Manyōshū* and in Shinran's religion of absolute other-power. These two seem to be opposites, and yet I too think they can be unified through Shinran's "effortless acceptance of the grace of Amida." Each seems to have a spiritual affinity with the mystical beauty of the *Genji monogatari* and the elegant simplicity of Bashō's haiku as well.

Heretofore, however, the Japanese spirit has been too insular; its sense of the ordinary and everyday has been superficial, and vainly self-confident. At this juncture, it must come to possess an acute Dostoievskian spirit in an eschatological sense, as the Japanese spirit participating in world history. In this way, it can become a point of departure for a new global culture.

The greatness of Dostoievski is that he saw mankind in its "vanishing point." The Dostoievskian spirit, however, does not wholly coincide with the religious sense of the ordinary and everyday. Here there is perhaps a difference between things Russian and things Japanese. And yet, I think that until Dostoievski's spirit is conjoined with a religious sense of common human experience, it will not realize its full potential. It will remain imprisoned in the standpoint of objectivity, of object logic.

Now this religious quality of common human experience is not be to confused with what philosophers have written about under the heading of "common sense." Common sense refers merely to social patterns of consciousness crystallized through custom and tradition. It is "habit" formed into human temperament. My religious concept of common experience refers rather to the self's immanent existential ground. It refers to the stand point from which the personal self becomes its own personal and unique self. It refers, in other words, to the dimension of absolute free will. (I repeat that this is the opposite of the Kantian idea of a merely formal will, too.)

True free will arises from the unbounded standpoint that is attained when the self is overturned through its own self-nega-tion, and thereby is attained an affirmation of the self which mir-rors the absolute's own self-negation. It is in this religious self-affirmation that we encounter the alpha and omega of the world, which are conversely the alpha and omega of ourselves. In a word, our consciousness of the absolute present is grounded in it. Therefore if we call it deep, it is utterly deep, penetrating to the very depths of the world. If we call it shallow, it is utterly shallow, having nothing underneath it. Point to it and it goes away, and yet it holds everything in its embrace.

I say, therefore, that everyday human existence has to be seen eschatologically. It is awareness of the absolute present. It is from that standpoint that we can conceive of a beginningless past and an endless future. History is not intelligible from the perspec-tive of the abstract conscious self. The latter is only the stand-point of autobiography. It is because there is always this eschato-logical quality in ordinary experience that we can speak of the contradictory identity of time and space, of the immanent and transcendent, that constitutes the creative process of history.

Western philosophy has developed on the basis of abstract logic. It represents the standpoint of abstract free will, and not of this common experience that is religious in character. Moreover, its concept of "common sense" must be distinguished from this common experience as well. Still, there is a common thread between the two concepts, since wherever there is the standpoint of the religiously everyday, "common sense" also appears. In this respect, I am interested in the French concept of *bon sens*. (See Montaigne's discussion of Socrates in this light in his *De la phy-siogomie*, III, 12.)

The most concrete standpoint of the self is that which is deepest and yet shallowest, largest and yet smallest—that is, ordinary experience that is religious in character. This is also Pas-cal's standpoint of *roseau pensant*.

Those who take the standpoint of Kantian philosophy maintain that cognition obtains when what is given in sensuous immediacy is formed by abstract logical categories of the understanding. In these constructive epistemological terms they hold that science begins from the negation of common sense. I say, however, that merely to negate the immediately given, and to move away from sensuous intuition by applying the abstract logical categories of the understanding, is not the path to truth. Objective cognition presupposes that the beginning and end of the cognitive process are always one experience. Kant himself, more than his later followers, stressed this kind of synthesis of the categories with sensuous immediacy. What is most true is that which is very far and yet very near. Truth arises from that standpoint where the point of departure of cognition is not lost at any point; truth always returns to its point of departure in the immediately given. I formulate this position in my concept of active intuition.

Now "common sense" is still a form of *doxa*, an "opinion" that can always be negated. But the religious quality of everyday experience is also present in common sense. That is why both cognition and moral practice arise from and are returnable to common sense. (I grant that this concept of common sense remains only a preliminary sketch.) What pertains to this common sensibility is prior to the determinations of the true and the good. Hence what ought to be negated is not intuition itself but "opinion." Even Newton's physics, which became the cornerstone of the vast development of modern physical science, if seen from the dynamically human standpoint of ordinary experience, turns out to have been only an "opinion," as present-day relativity and quantum mechanics are bringing out. Newton conceives of absolute time and space—absolutes that are relative to the human act of measuring. The French physicist Paul Langevin (1872–1946) has indicated that the quantum theory does not negate determinism, but only makes it more humanly and concretely precise.

Religious awareness involves realizing the Archimedean point of the historical world's eternal past and eternal future, the beginning and end of mankind, in the very present itself. It involves realizing the unity of what is very far and yet very near, the greatest and the smallest—the dimension of ordinary experience itself.

The religious form of life is that dimension of experience in which human existence itself comes into focus. It does not have a fixed content. It is the standpoint of all standpoints. Every claim of privileged content for it becomes mere superstition. Hence religious creeds must always be taken as only symbolic. Religious creeds are only the immediate expressions of our historical life. With that qualification, religious symbols have their significance. But the goal of true religion should lie in grasping eternal life in its own immediacy in our lives. That is why it is in ordinary experience that "the Dharma-body is just myself, Makabe Hcishirō." In it all standpoints are negated, and yet from it all standpoints arise.

The religious standpoint, I say, is the standpoint that is not a standpoint. And yet from it appears an endless stream of "great wisdom and great practice." Therefore it is written: "One drop from the source of Sōgen [a reference to the sixth Zen patriarch, Hui-neng] will enable one to enjoy enlightenment without end." The perspectives of the true, the good, and the beautiful are all, in my view, grounded in this religious form of life.

Religion is often called mystical. But when I speak of religion, I do not refer to a special kind of consciousness. "There is no mysterious power in the true Dharma"—the mystical has no use at all in our practical lives. Were religion some special consciousness of privileged persons it would merely be the idle matter of idle men. "The true Way cannot exist apart even for an instant; what can do so is not the true Way." Again, "When we run, we are on the true Way; when we stumble and fall, we are still on it." Religion is not apart from common experience. "The ordinary mind is the Way," in Nan-ch'üan's words.

In religious experience one penetrates to the depths of one's own everyday experience. The self, as the self-determination of the absolute present, always faces the absolute in this way. The self is, eschatologically, continuous with the world's beginning and end, at each and every step of its life. Therefore Nan-ch'üan is also quoted as saying: "Even to set upon the quest for awakening is to go astray." And when he was asked if one does not set upon the quest, how can the Way be found, he replied: "The Way does not pertain to finding or not-finding." Religion arises precisely from that attitude.

Religion, therefore, is not simply an event within the individual consciousness. It must be the self-awareness of historical life. That is why every religion has originated historically and socially out of folk belief. The founders of the religions were those who thoroughly expressed the folk beliefs of their respective cultures. They may be called the mouths of God, as were the prophets of Israel. Without the expressiveness of this self-transforming world, historical societies would not arise in the first place. Accordingly, every historically crystallized society begins from a religious ground—from what Durkeim has called *le sacré*. But religious beliefs rise and fall with the fortunes of nations. The national religions of the Greeks and the Romans perished with them. True religion, however, does not exist for the sake of some special nation. The reason that a nation is a nation lies, in the first place, in its religious character as a self-expression of historical life. A true nation arises when a people harbors the world-principle within itself and forms itself historically and socially.

The religion of Yahweh, too, was originally a folk religion of the Jewish race. The Jews, by transcending their merely ethnic belief, deepened and elevated it into a world religion. Even during the time when they lost their native land as slaves of the Babylonians, they never lost their religion. They never lost their spiritual self-confidence, as it were. Their self-confidence as God's chosen people did not lie in military prowess and glory. Their religious awareness was deepened and elevated by the prophets such as Jeremiah, Ezechiel, and the second Isaiah. Jeremiah was a thorough patriot. Still, he warned his people by calling Nebuchadnezzar the servant of Yahweh.

The historical world, as the self-determination of the absolute, exists in the form of the absolute present. Therefore, as the contradictory identity of that which expresses and that which is expressed, the historical world, as the expression of the self-expressive absolute, contains its own self-expression within itself and transforms itself in this way. For this reason the historical world is religious, and is metaphysical, in essence. Every race of people, as a formation of the historical world, is its own expression of God.

From this standpoint, there is a distinction between a mere biological species and a race of people as a historical species. A race of people is not merely a species in the biological sense. Even if the life-world is biological, the self-expression of the historical world lies at its foundation. When the blood of a race begins to form its own expression of itself, that race becomes a historical species. But as Ranke puts it, there is not only one historical race. Such an idea is merely an abstraction. In the dawn of history, the human world was predominantly spatial. The races existed in spatial contemporaneity, or merely side by side, as it were. The world of the absolute present, dormant in its temporal axis, was not yet self-transforming and the human world was not yet world-historical.

Yet the historical world becomes concrete through a process of dynamic transformation. It comes to possess its own expressive centers within itself. It grows, as it were, from something two-dimensional to three-dimensional. It is only in this process that the historical world is realized; only here does the historical world realize itself. The content of the historical world's self-transformation is culture; and the religious always functions as its ground. Thus the global human world, by transcending the merely racial, has come to have its identity in the world religions. Christianity, after developing from a Jewish folk belief into a world religion, played such a role in medieval European culture. Such a global concept has never crystallized to a comparable degree in the East. But it would seem that both Buddhism and the Confucian ritual teachings of China have played the roles of world religions in the East. It is said, for example, that in the Spring and Autumn period (722–481 B.C.), China and the barbarians were distinguished according to the criterion of ritual.

A global humanity is formed when the historical world, as the self-determination of the absolute present, transcends its racial particularities. In that instance, the old worlds lose their specific traditions, become anti-individual, abstractly universal, anti-religious, and scientific. We see this process of secularization in the "progress" of modern European culture. As the absolute's affirmation through its own negation, such a negative moment contributes to the direction of the world's transformation. Now that which negates the human is also contained in the historical world. But the absolute does not transcend the relative. The true absolute must possess its own negation. Consequently the relative is not merely the abstract form of the absolute, but is the absolute's own negation. There is always this contradictory identity of the many and the one. And therefore the negation of the old worlds is included within the historical world's self-formative development. It is through this kind of self-negation that the world exists and moves through itself, and is absolutely real.

The mere form of self-negation, of course, is not reality that exists and moves by itself. The physical world answers to just such an abstraction. But the world of science is still a human product, even as a form of the historical world's self-negation. Therefore science is also a form of culture. Mankind is scientific from that standpoint where it possesses itself in self-negation. In religious language, it is the fact that God sees himself through his own self-negation. In this sense the world of science may also be said to be religious. Kepler's astronomy, for example, is said to have been religious in inspiration. From the abstractly theoretical standpoint of scientific discourse, God possesses himself through self-negation. We can also speak, in Hegel's terms, of the world of the spirit that is alienated from itself.

I should like to clarify the relation between religion and culture in this context. Religion and culture can be conceived of as opposite standpoints in one respect. Present-day dialectical theology has been stressing this view as a reaction against the tendency to identify the two. I think, however, that a God who does not empty himself, a God who does not express himself through his own self-negation, is not the true absolute. This might be a God who sits in judgment, but not the God of absolute mercy. It might be a God who is transcendent Lord, but not the immanent God of absolute love. True culture arises as the content of the paradox of God, of God's own self-affirmation through self-negation. From this human perspective, truly objective, eternal cultural content appears in the self-negation of the human—that is, in the dimension in which the self possesses itself in that which transcends it, and yet functions as a transformative vector of the historical world. A culture is the content of a form forming itself as a self-determination of the absolute present. In contrast to the dialectical theologians, therefore, I assert that true culture is religious and true religion is cultural. A religion that merely negates culture would not be truly religious. It would be a religion without content, a mere negation of the human; it would be merely transcendent. The religion of God understood as transcendent Lord has at times been prone to degenerate in this way. Therefore, while I have always been sympathetic to the position that affirms the transcendent nature of religion held by contemporary dialectical theology, in opposition to the merely immanent and rational view of religion in past thinkers, I cannot help recognizing a respect in which it is reactionary.

Now when I say here that true religion must be cultural, I do not mean to conceive of religion as identical with culture. I do not derive religion in merely rational and immanent terms. There can be no religion in merely immanent human terms. Religion must be immanently transcendent and transcendently immanent. Religion comes into focus from the standpoint of the absolutely contradictory identity, the dynamic equilibrium, of immanence and transcendence.

Religion has in the past been grasped in terms of the logic of the grammatical subject. Accordingly, it has been taken as something mystical. The various misunderstandings and imperfect conceptions of religion are returnable to that logic. I contend, however, that a logic of religion as a form of the historical world must be absolutely dialectical. I say that even Hegel's logic falls short of this. To consider religion only in rational terms drawn from the immanent human world is to negate religion. In this negation of religion the world loses itself, and mankind likewise loses itself and denies its true selfhood. For mankind has essentially a self-contradictory existence, as I have indicated.

I assert, therefore, that a true culture must be religious, and a true religion must be cultural. We see *Deus absconditus* in the background of a true culture.

When mankind, however, maximizes the human standpoint in a non-religious form, in a purely secular direction, the result is that the world negates itself and mankind loses itself. This has been the trend of European culture since the Renaissance, and the reason that such a thing as the decline and fall of the West has been proclaimed. When the world loses itself and human beings come to forget God, mankind becomes boundlessly individual and selfish. The world then becomes mere play or struggle, and the possibility of a true culture is undermined. The condition of mere secular culture ultimately loses all sense of true culture.

In recent times some thinkers, distressed over the future of European culture, have been advocating a return to the middle ages. (I cite Christopher Dawson, for one example.) Yet, although it may roughly be said that history runs in cycles, it in fact never repeats itself. Each epoch of history is a new creation. Modern culture has developed from medieval culture by its own historical necessity. It is not possible to return to the standpoint of medieval culture; nor can medieval culture be the factor that saves modern culture. A new cultural direction has now to be sought. A new mankind must be born.

Christianity, which formed the center of self-consciousness in the medieval world, was a religion that experienced transcendence in an objective direction. It was a religion of God as the transcendent Lord. In this way it fused with secular institutions. The successors of Peter also became the successors of Caesar. Such a religion must negate itself. For what is of Caesar must be rendered unto Caesar. Religion does not exist behind the sword of Caesar. As something formed, such a world yields to the forming, by historical necessity. Paul Tillich writes that Protestantism regards nature as the place of decision. We must always progress in that direction. In other words, we advance in the direction that sees God as self-negation. But to move in a merely immanent human direction would again result in the world's losing itself and mankind's negating itself.

I thus maintain that we must proceed by the logic of absolutely contradictory identity—that is, of transcending immanently. This immanent transcendence is the road to a new global culture.

In this sense I am interested in the dramatic poem of Ivan Karamazov. Moved to sympathy for mankind that laments, "O Lord, show your face to us," Christ again descends to the human world. The place is Seville, in Spain. The time is the fifteenth century, when men are daily being burned at the stake "for the glory of God." It is the time of the horrible Inquisition. The bishop who is the Grand Inquisitor, seeing Christ perform another miracle, suddenly darkens his face and orders the guards to arrest Christ and throw him into prison. He torments Christ with the following interrogation:

For what reason have you come again? You seem now to have nothing to say. The freedom of mankind was of primary importance to you fifteen hundred years ago. Did you not say, "I wish to make you free"? You see now the form of their freedom. We have completed this work in your name. The people now believe more strongly than ever that they have become free. But they go on sacrificing their freedom to us. They meekly place their freedom under our feet. It is we who have accomplished this. As for what you had hoped for, there must not be any such thing; there must be no such freedom.

In short, the Grand Inquisitor says that they have made men happy by conquering their freedom. There is nothing more difficult for humans to endure than their own freedom. Saying that mankind does not live by bread alone, Christ rejected the way of the world. But unfortunately, when Christ left this world, he passed his work to the Roman popes. Today he cannot abrogate their authority. They say to him: "Why have you come to bother us? Tomorrow you shall be burned at the stake!"

To this, Christ never says a word. He is as silent as a shadow. When released the next day, still silent, he suddenly approaches the old Inquisitor and kisses him. The old man is shocked.

This Christ, who from beginning to end is silent as a shadow, seems to me to be an immanently transcendent Christ. Of course, Christians, even Dostoievski himself, may not say this. It is my private interpretation. But it may be that a new Christian world will begin through an immanently transcendent Christ. It would be anachronistic to return to the middles ages. Perhaps taking our cue from Shinran's effortless acceptance of the grace of Amida, we will find the true God in the place where there is no God. From the perspective of present-day global history, it will perhaps be Buddhism that contributes to the formation of the new historical age. But if it too is only the conventional Buddhism of bygone days, it will merely be a relic of the past. The universal religions, insofar as they are already crystallized, have distinctive features corresponding to the times and the places of the races that formed them. While each thus partakes of the essence of religion, none has exhausted it. The religion of the future, I think, will evolve in the direction of the immanently transcendent rather than the transcendently immanent.

For this reason I am generally sympathetic with the direction of Berdyaev's *The Meaning of History*, but his philosophy does not go beyond the mysticism of Boehme. The new age must primarily be scientific. Paul Tillich's *Kairos und Logos* also agrees with my epistemology, but his logic remains unclear. These new directions must now be given a thoroughgoing logical foundation.

I have touched upon the relation between nations and religion from the fourth volume of my *Philosophical Essays*. Each nation is a world that contains the self-expression of the absolute within itself. Hence I say that when a racial society harbors the world's self-expression within itself—when it becomes rational— it becomes a nation. This is the prerequisite of nationhood. In this sense, the nation is religious. The form of the historical world's self-formation that is religious in its ground is that of the nation.

The historical world realizes itself in the form of nations. Yet I do not say that the nation itself is the absolute. The nation is the fountainhead of morality, but not of religion. As the nation is a form of the absolute's own self-formation, our moral actions must reflect a national character; but the nation does not save our souls. The true nation has its ground in the religious. A religious person, in his moral behavior, must naturally be a citizen of a nation as something historically formative. And yet the two standpoints must always be distinguished as well. If they are not, the pure development of each, religion and morality, will be obstructed, regressing into the "medieval" identity of the two. This is the reason modern nations have come to recognize freedom of religious belief over against the authority of the political state. A fusion of the Christianity of God as Lord with the nation may easily be contemplated; but this is less easily contemplated with respect to Buddhism, which in the past has even been regarded as apolitical.

In closing, let me cite Suzuki's comments on the passage of the *Sukhavativyuha Sutra* which says, "All four groups of the earthly congregation were then able to see all that was on the other side instantly. And those in the Pure Land saw this land, too, just as the former saw them." Suzuki interprets this to mean that just as the assembled throngs in this world, who take veneration of the Buddha as the center of their religious life, see the Pure Land, so too this world is seen by the assembled throngs who have already attained the Pure Land. This corrupt world reflects the Pure Land, and the Pure Land reflects this corrupt world. They are mutually reflecting mirrors. This points to the interconnectedness, or oneness, of the Pure Land and this corrupt world. I think I am able to conceive of the nation in these terms. The nation is the mirror image of the Pure Land in this world.

Concerning My Logic

As the result of my cogitations over these many long years, I think I have been able to clarify the form of thinking—that is, the logic—of the historically formative act from the standpoint of the historically active self itself. I have endeavored to consider as well, through my logic, various questions fundamental to the natural sciences, and to morals and religion. I think, moreover, that I have succeeded in framing questions that have never been properly framed from the standpoints of previous logics. At least, I think I have been able to indicate the path along which further clarification can come.

The reason this path has not been taken is that past logics have tended to remain without sufficient grounding. From the standpoint of abstract logic, the concrete cannot even be considered. My logic, however, has not been understood by the academic world—indeed, I may say that it has not yet been given the slightest serious consideration. Not that there hasn't been criticism. But the kind of criticism it has received has distorted my meaning—merely criticizing by objectifying my standpoint from its own. It has not been a criticism from within my own standpoint. A criticism from a different standpoint which does not truly understand what it is criticizing cannot be said to be a true criticism. I seek, above all, an understanding of what I am saying from my own standpoint.

Some people will say that my logic of contradictory identity is not a logic. They may dismiss it as a religious experience. I ask them, however—what is logic? There is probably no one who will deny that Aristotle's logic is a logic. Kant states that after Aristotle logic neither retreated nor advanced a single step—that logic appears to have been perfected by Aristotle. Now Aristotle's logic is the form of the linguistic self-expression of the world which expresses itself in symbolic forms; in that respect it may be said to be a logic in the finest sense. Moreover, we could say that logic in this sense was perfected by Aristotle. But let us add that the transcendental logic of the very same Kant, who says this of Aristotle's logic, is no longer the logic of Aristotle!

Furthermore, when we turn to Hegel's logic—that is, dialectical logic—we find that it even seems to entail the negation of Aristotle's logic. In Aristotle, contradiction cannot be the very form of logic. But in Hegel's logic, contradiction is precisely the discursive form of logic's own self-development. Now can't we say that Kant's and Hegel's logics are indeed logics, each in its own way? If we take this question seriously, we have to rethink the whole question of what logic is. Logic is the discursive form of our thinking. And we will only be able to clarify what logic is by reflecting on the form of our own thinking.

Postscript
Nishida's Logic of the East

As we have seen, Nishida came to forge a powerful tool with which to articulate the existential structure of the religious consciousness. This tool was precisely that of the "logic of contradictory identity," which he identified with the logic of Nāgārjuna and the East Asian Buddhist traditions. He saw it, for example, as the common logic of the Zen and Pure Land schools. This explicit identification of his method of discursive operation with the Buddhist traditions, however, is a comparatively late development in Nishida's writings. It does not clearly surface until around 1939, and then only briefly at the conclusion of one of his *Philosophical Essays*.[1] It does not come emphatically into focus until Nishida's essay on Leibniz's concept of preestablished harmony in 1944, and finally in the "Religious Worldview" essay of 1945.

Meanwhile, of course, Nishida had been working with the "logic" *(ronri)* of "the place of nothingness" *(mu no basho)* since 1927. In his preface to the pivotal work *Hataraku mono kara miru mono e* (From Acting to Seeing), published in that year, he states explicitly that his thought is undergoing a radical turn. This philosophical metanoesis involves, he says, a shift from the kind of Fichtean voluntarism that had occupied him for the previous ten years to a new kind of intuitionism articulated in terms of "the place of nothingness." At that critical juncture, namely 1927, Nishida was content to associate this new articulation with "the form of the formless, the voice of the voiceless, which lies at the basis of Eastern culture, transmitted from our ancestors for thousands of years."[2]

Let us briefly recapitulate the significance of this announced metanoesis in 1927. Nishida's early writings indicate that he had been first drawn to the "pure experience" doctrine of William

James and the *élan vital* concept of Bergson, and thereafter to Fichte's doctrine of the creative moral will. Nishida experimented with ways of articulating the latter's doctrine, with its cardinal concept of self-positing activity *(Tathandlung)*, as the metaphysical ground of Neo-Kantian and Husserlian concepts of the transcendental ego.[3] At the same time these early writings reveal his continued interest in the Christian Neo-Platonists, especially the mystical theologians Erigena, Eckhart, Boehme, and Cusanus. And again, Nishida's early text assimilates ideas from philosophers as diverse and incompatible as Berkeley, Hegel, and Schopenhauer. Fichte's *Tathandlung* remained the grounding concept for Nishida for a good ten years, between 1917 and 1927, when he was at the height of his academic career. Only as he was retiring from his official academic post in 1927 did he announce that he was displacing Fichte's *Tathandlung* with the deeper a priori of the active existential self—that religiously self-conscious self which paradoxically sees without being a seer.

For the next seven or eight years Nishida worked out a number of dimensions and ramifications of this "logic of the place of nothingness" *(mu no bashoteki ronri)* in relation to fundamental philosophical problems drawn from such major Western philosophers as Aristotle, Descartes, Kant, Fichte, Schelling, Hegel, Marx, and Husserl. Entirely absent in his Fichtean period, the language of "contradictory identity" *(mujunteki dōitsu)* becomes ubiquitous, and semantically pivotal, in his post-1927 writings. But Nishida continued to describe his new logic as "dialectical" *(benshōhō teki)* in several of his ensuing volumes of publications. For example, he now called his logic "absolutely dialectical" in contrast to the "merely immanentistic" dialectics of Hegel or of Marx.[4] Only gradually, between 1935 and 1945, did he come to favor the language of "contradictory identity" over that of "dialectical." Even when he continued to employ the term "dialectical" he meant it in the paradoxical, as distinguished from the sublational, sense. This potential confusion (to the reader) will only be cleared up by a detailed study of Nishida's writings from 1927 through 1945.

It should be noted that these years, between 1927 and 1945, coincided with the rise of ultranationalistic ideologies in Japan. Nishida's thought as a whole remained remarkably free of those ideological currents despite the attempt of the authorities to coopt his name on occasion. If anything, Nishida's text may be rather atypical in that respect.[5] Nevertheless a comparatively mild strain of chauvinistic definition does appear in Nishida's writings during those years. It is only a *leitmotif* in the overall corpus of his writings—a *leitmotif* which pridefully celebrates "the form of the formless, the voice of the voiceless, which lies at the basis of Eastern culture, transmitted from our ancestors for thousands of years."

This strain of definition, which gradually crystalized in Nishida's own articulation of a "logic of the East" *(tōyōteki ronri)* and an "Asian nothingness" *(tōyōteki mu)*, has been further accentuated in the culturally prideful, and yet also apologetic, pronouncements of the Kyoto School followers of Nishida.[6] Nishida's text as a whole, and especially his "Religious World-view" essay of 1945, represents such a monumental engagement of the positions of Western philosophy that it can be said to have established the conceptual framework, and authoritative back-drop, for the subsequent "encounter theology" of the Kyoto School. Yet what seems to be the case is that the Kyoto School has availed itself of the rhetorically charged concept of "Asian noth-ingness" for the purpose of engaging in encounter theology while at the same time showing little inclination to employ or develop Nishida's complicated conceptual analyses.[7]

Thus the very dynamic of Nishida's logic has lent itself to a domain of discourse that has centered on theological (or Buddho-logical) confrontation of "East" and "West." The reason for this is not far to seek. In its internal movement the logic of contradic-tory identity takes shape as a tensional opposition without synthesis, as in the concept of the nonduality of nirvana and sam-sara. The same logic, when turned outwardly to confront diver-gent positions, proceeds to structure such differences according to a rule of disparity. The differences are reduced to an unresolva-ble tension between "concrete" and "abstract" logics, for exam-ple—or to the disparity between "Eastern" and "Western" forms of culture and metaphysics.[8] Internally paradoxical, externally confrontational—that is the deconstructive dynamic of this mode of discursive operation. Although the precedent for this refuta-tional thrust can be traced all the way back to Nāgārjuna's *Mula-*

madhyamikakarika,[9] we need only mention other, non-Asian examples of the use of this logical operator to confirm the present characterization. A doubly adversative methodic procedure does in fact prevail in the texts of Heraclitus, the Greek Sophists (as reported in Plato's dialogues), Kierkegaard, Nietzsche, Wittgenstein, and the contemporary French writer Jacques Derrida, among others.[10]

Because he was committed to this paradoxical form of articulation at a presuppositional level, even Nishida underestimated the potential for structural—that is, cross-cultural—analysis which his own writings so vividly suggest. Take, for example, his interest in the "absolute paradox" language of Kierkegaard, which Nishida weaves into his own discourse on the religious consciousness. Internally, the texts of Kierkegaard and Nishida both employ the paradoxical mode to articulate the "presence and absence" of the absolute and the relative; externally, they both proceed to "confront" the dialectical Subject of Hegel in no uncertain terms. This semantic affinity serves to undermine the East-West "difference" which Nishida's text elsewhere proposes. We have seen numerous other revelations of affine, cross-cultural linkages in Nishida's text. Most notably, Nishida aligns his thinking about the nondual identity of the absolute and the relative with that of the apophatic mystical theologians Erigena, Eckhart, Boehme, and Cusanus. If anything, these cross-cultural analyses are one of the strengths of Nishida's text.

We have also seen that the paradoxical mode reduces to the basic predicative structure of "is *and yet* is not." We can alternately characterize this as the logic of the simultaneity, and biconditionality, of opposites without their higher synthesis. Thus "is" if, and only if, "is not," as in the *soku hi* formulation. In Nāgārjuna's logic, the four positions $+1$, -1, $+1$ *and* -1, and *not* $(+1$ *and* $-1)$ all return to the same basic structure of biconditional opposition. That is, they return to $+1$ *and* -1 (or, -1 *and* $+1$). In the "negative version" of the same logical form, we get *not* $(+1)$, *not* (-1), *not* $(+1$ *and* $-1)$, and *not* (*not* $(+1$ *and* $-1)$). Factoring these values out will merely revert the logical form to the same biconditional symmetry of "is and yet is not"—that is, to $+1$ *and* -1 (or, -1 *and* $+1$). The "and" in these various formulations is always an "and yet" with its corresponding "vice versa." Nirvana and yet samsara; samsara and yet nirvana. Nirvana *(+1)* if, and only if, samsara *(-1)*; samsara *(-1)* if, and only if, nirvana *(+1)*. Thus the "nonduality" of nirvana and samsara semantically presupposes this type of logical structure. The *locus classicus* for Nāgārjuna, as well as for the whole Mahayana tradition and for Nishida, is the paradoxical verse of the *Prajnaparamita Sutra:* "form is emptiness, and emptiness is form." That is to say, "form is emptiness, and yet emptiness is form, and vice versa." Or, "form is emptiness if, and only if, emptiness is form, and vice versa." In providing an exhaustive set of the positive and negative possibilities of this paradoxical logical form, Nāgārjuna wrote the methodic script, as it were, for the traditions of Indian and East Asian Mahayana Buddhism. Nishida came to repossess this same logical form in a contemporary philosophical version.

It is crucial to repeat, however, that this is not a logic of Buddhism or a "logic of the East" in any proprietary sense. Plato's text, for one, repeatedly characterizes the logic of his philosophical rivals, the Sophists, as a logic of ambiguation—the very paradoxical logic of "is and yet is not" under discussion. (Plato's own discursive mode is dialectical, as he makes abundantly clear in the *Republic* and other dialogues.) Perhaps the *locus classicus* of this type of logic in Plato's writings is the *Parmenides*, which, in a manner reminiscent of Nāgārjuna, traces the operation of Sophistic logic through the variety of its possible forms. Plato has in mind not only the Sophists but the logic of Heraclitus, and of Parmenides and Zeno, as well. After exploring the eight or nine "hypotheses" of the paradoxical logic, Plato concludes the *Parmenides* with the words:

> To this we may add the conclusion. It seems that whether there is or is not a one, both that one and the others alike are and are not, and appear and do not appear to be, all manner of things in all manner of ways, with respect to themselves and to one another.[11]

In his *Appearance and Reality*, F. H. Bradley follows the same strategy as Plato's in the *Parmenides*. Book One, "Appearance," exhibits the paradoxical logic of the self-contradicting forms of terms and their relations while Book Two, "Reality," formulates a dialectical synthesis of the many in the One—Bradley's Absolute.[12] Both Plato and Bradley explicitly take cognizance of the "hypothetical" logic of $+1 \equiv -1$ only to reject it (or incorporate it) from the standpoint of their respective versions of the dialectical, or sublational, mode of articulation. Between Plato and Bradley, of course, there is Hegel, who was well aware of the paradoxical logical form.

Rejection of, as well as adherence to, versions of this paradoxical form can be observed along the entire spectrum of Eastern and Western philosophy. The logical operator subtending the classical Confucian texts, for example, is returnable to the tensional opposition between the "superior man" *(chün tzu)* and his moral and cultural counterpart, the "inferior man" *(hsiao jen)*. This kind of thinking is also exhibited in the literary and moral traditions of Japanese culture. But it is nothing "Eastern." A close structural parallel can be found in the theme of the irreducible opposition between the moralities of "good and bad" and "good and evil" which runs through Nietzsche's philosophical writings. In a broader analysis, the paradoxical, or agonistic, logical form will be seen as the common methodic procedure of the texts of the Greek Sophists and Skeptics, of classical Chinese Confucianism, of the good bishop Berkeley (that archsceptic and sophist in the eyes of David Hume),[13] and of Kierkegaard, Nietzsche, and Freud. It is conspicuously exhibited in the deconstructive writings of Jacques Derrida and other "postmoderns."

It is also evident that the paradoxical form of human utterance is to be found ubiquitously in the literary traditions of the world. To be sure, it is a prevailing feature of Japanese literary style, from the *Genji monogatari* through the *haiku* of Matsuo Bashō to the novels of Kawabata Yasunari. The delicate sense of contradiction *(mujun)*, for example, is typically exhibited in the *Genji monogatari* in the passage in chapter 52, "The Drake Fly," which reads:

> So his thoughts returned always to the same family. As he sank deeper in memories of Uji, cruel ties with the Uji family, drake flies, than which no creatures are more fragile and insubstantial, were flitting back and forth in the evening light.
>
> "I see the drake fly, take it up in my hand. Ah, here it is—and it is gone."
>
> And he added softly, as always: "here, and perhaps not here at all."[14]

"Here, and perhaps not here at all" is the discursive mode in which the poignant meaning of this text is crystallized. It is a version of the logic of "is and is not," as presence and absence, which runs through the sensibility expressed in the *Kokinshū*, the *Shinkokinshū*, and other traditional Japanese poetic anthologies. Scholars of Japanese culture have not failed to point out the close relation between this aesthetic sensibility and the religious sensibility of such writers as Kūkai, Dōgen, and Musō Soseki.

For another example, the *Makurazōshi* of Sei Shōnagaon, a contemporary of the author of the *Genji monogatari*, is a virtual thesaurus of paradoxical, and erotically tinged, statements. Among them is this entry:

Things That Are Near, but Far

Amida's paradise,
The ship's course,
The relation between a man and a woman.[15]

If we turn to another tradition, we find the works of the Elizabethan and Jacobean poets and dramatists to be replete with instances of the paradoxical, or agonistic, form of articulation.[16] (The tension of opposites is played out on a grander, religious scale in the poetry of John Milton.) For our present purposes let us cite Shakespeare's "The Phoenix and the Turtle" as an outstanding example of a poetic rendering of the logic of nonduality.

Here the anthem doth commence:
Love and constancy is dead;
Phoenix and the Turtle fled
In a mutual flame from hence.

So they lov'd, as love in twain
Had the essence but in one;
Two distincts, division none;
Number there in love was slain.

Hearts remote, yet not asunder;
Distance and no space was seen
'Twixt this Turtle and his queen:
But in them it were a wonder.

So between them love did shine,
That the Turtle saw his right

Flaming in the Phoenix' sight;
Either was the other's mine.

Property was thus appalled
That the self was not the same;
Single nature's double name
Neither two nor one was called.

Reason, in itself confounded,
Saw division grow together,
To themselves yet neither either,
Simple were so well compounded:

That it cried, How true a twain
Seemeth this concordant one!
Love hath reason, reason none,
If what parts, can so remain.[17]

It is almost as if Shakespeare had studied the logic of Nāgārjuna or
the eight or nine hypotheses of Plato's *Parmenides* before composing these extraordinary verses.

Among the many literary examples that could be cited, one
more will have to suffice. The twentieth-century American poet
Wallace Stevens inscribes a beautiful version of the logic of contradictory identity in his "Notes Toward a Supreme Fiction":

Two things of opposite natures seem to depend
On one another, as a man depends
On a woman, day on night, the imagined

On the real. This is the origin of change.
Winter and spring, cold copulars, embrace
And forth the particulars of rapture come.

Music falls on the silence like a sense,
A passion that we feel, not understand.
Morning and afternoon are clasped together

And North and South are an intrinsic couple
And sun and rain a plural, like two lovers
That walk away as one in the greenest body.

In solitude the trumpets of solitude
Are not of another solitude resounding;
A little string speaks for a crowd of voices.

The partaker partakes of that which changes him.
The child that touches takes character from the thing,
The body, it touches. The captain and his men

Are one and the sailor and the sea are one.
Follow after, O my companion, my fellow, my self,
Sister and solace, brother and delight.[18]

Stevens' poem, too, resonates in uncanny ways not only with the verses of Shakespeare's "The Phoenix and the Turtle" but with the paradoxically articulated texts of Heraclitus, of Mahayana Buddhists, and of Nishida.

Returning to our comparative philosophical analysis, we can observe that the same generic logical form, with numerous species and subspecies, subtends philosophical texts on a global scale.[19] The *leitmotif* in Nishida's writings that plays off "East" against "West" is itself a version of this logic of opposites without synthesis.

In contrast with this paradoxical form of articulation, we also find numerous instances of the dialectical, or sublational, mode of operation. For example, the sublational method is common to the texts of Hinduism and Taoism as well as of Pythagoras, Plato, Plotinus, and the Christian Neo-Platonists; of Fichte, Schelling, Hegel, and Marx; of Royce, Bradley, Bergson, Whitehead, Heidegger, and even of Sartre. It is, again, the form of rationality of the major Neo-Confucian texts, such as of the Chu Hsi and Wang Yang-ming schools of China and Japan.

Now dialectical and agonistic methods of articulation have been self-consciously counterposed by philosophers throughout the global history of thought and spirituality. Thus we have Hinduism and Buddhism; Plato and the Sophists; Plato and Heraclitus; Neo-Confucianists and Buddhists; Hegel and Kierkegaard; Heidegger and Derrida, and so on. In the light of these historical interactions it is relevant to point out once again that Nishida's own claim to a "logic of the East" encourages a confrontational attitude when it differentiates between his "concrete logic" of contradictory identity and the "abstract" logics of Aristotle, Kant, and Hegel. Indeed, he reiterated this contention when he penned his *zeppitsu* ("final words") just two or three days before his death. In it he assesses the logics of Aristotle, Kant, and Hegel

according to a rule of disparity while turning Hegel's claim to
having articulated the truly "concrete logic" against all three of
the Western philosophers.[20]

Given the fact that philosophers have so confronted their
peers, the hermeneutical question becomes the obvious one of
how to discern the types of logic that have been employed in the
history of philosophical texts. This problem will also be seen to
subtend the question whether Nishida's own logic can serve as
the foundational method of discrimination of such types. At the
least, we must ask whether an agonistic method, which counter-
poses "Eastern" and "Western" forms of logic and ontology according to a rule of disparity, or according to a principle of tensional opposition, is the most suitable form in which to pursue
cross-cultural analyses. It may even be the case that the possibility of eidetic intuition of cross-cultural structures, as semantological variables, is undermined by the very presuppositions of the
logic of "is and is not" itself.

A related question is whether Nishida's analysis, for all its
attention to the several "abstract" logics of Aristotle, Kant, and
Hegel, provides us with a complete set of the logical forms of
philosophical discourse. Until we have an exhaustive set, archi-
tectonically exhibited as constituting an essential variety of
types, it will be impossible to adjudicate Nishida's own claims.
But of course, Nishida's assertion of the difference between "concrete" and "abstract" logics foredooms the possibility of such an
adjudication. For a discursive method that discriminates an essential variety of types would be prejudged by his own logic of disparity. To Nishida, as to Jacques Derrida, the very notion of a
complete set would break up into the play of cultural "differences."

The analogy here with Derrida's contemporary hermeneutic
may serve to shed light on Nishida's project in several significant
respects. Derrida's text is committed in principle to the prolifera-
tion of textual differences—to an interminable play of signifiers
in the interpretive process. But this is no merely arbitrary game.
Derridean interpretation must proceed according to its own formal rules. The reading and/or writing supplement must be rigor-
ously prescribed "by certain necessities of the game"—that is to
say, "by the logic of the play, signs to which the system of all tex-

tual powers must be accorded and attuned."[21] Or again: "Textuality being constituted by differences and by differences from differences, it is by nature absolutely heterogeneous and is constantly composing with the forces that tend to annihilate it."[22] The texts of cultures—or perhaps more precisely, the texts in which we interpret cultures—would fall under the same differential rubric. If we follow Derrida's logic, no cultural twain shall ever meet in our texts.

Like all good philosophical texts, Derrida's legislates its own discursive form in an assertive mode and acts out the same form in its textual performance. But given its methodic hardwires, so to speak, Derrida's text can only legitimately operate in a dyadic structure. It is constrained to do so by its own two-voiced logic of *differance*, which situates it at the adversative edge of presence and absence in the play of textual significations. There can be no question as to the specific semantic effect which such a hermeneutical instrument entails. Always operating in the cracks of the dyadic logical form, it becomes sense-making in its own deconstructive fashion.

But in another text, and from another perspective, we can ask whether Derrida's logic of *differance*, despite its good intentions of liberating the hidden energies of texts, is not ultimately procrustean in its effect. For precisely because Derrida's logic of *differance* entails a discursive procedure that is dynamically adversative, it proceeds to read the "software"—here, the variety of philosophical texts with their several semantic integrities—through its own kind of polarizing filter.

Here let us pause to disambiguate the concept of polarization before going further. We have seen that there are two kinds of textual logical operators that function in a two-voiced form—the dialectical and the agonistic. The dialectical form sublates antithetical terms in a higher, concrete synthesis. The agonistic form constitutes the tension between antithetical terms without their higher synthesis. Both are methodic forms which are broadly asserted and exhibited in the world-history of philosophy. The assertion and defense of either form always takes place in a text which exhibits (or "acts out") the preferred form in its own discursive procedure. The texts of Hegel and Derrida are cases in point. It is important to observe, however, that polarization of concepts occurs in both formal semantic procedures.

In the terms of our present analysis, the Derridean textual strategy involves a fundamental "mis-take" in methodological procedure. For the basic unit of philosophical signification—and therefore of analysis as well—is the *individual text*, not traditions of texts. It is individual philosophers who legislate for human reason; and manifestly, individual philosophers differ from one another in fundamental ways. Their radical differences, however, can only with the greatest disingenuity be reduced to a two-voiced adversative form of taxonomy. Nor again can traditions of texts—including, but not limited to, cultural traditions of texts—be cast in a mold of wholesale polarization. For if individual philosophical texts remain internally consistent (or homoarchic) in their semantic performances, traditions of texts do not necessarily do so. Nor do we apply the same standard of internal consistency to a tradition of texts that we do apply to an individual text.

It seems fair to say that the more long-lasting a cultural tradition and the wider its geographical scope, the more likely it will be to exhibit heteroarchic or essential differences among its major texts. A careful scrutiny of the Western, Indian, Chinese, or Japanese cultural traditions will yield a rich multiplicity of immortal texts, each with its own exemplary worldview. Such an examination, moreover, will generally uncover an irreducible variety of subaltern traditions. Therefore to speak of overarching traditions of texts—and to polarize them into "Eastern" and "Western" in the extreme case—is one of the shortest routes to the deconstruction, not to say obfuscation, of the authentic philosophical meanings of individual texts. It is an effective rhetorical strategy, to be sure, in the service of a wholesale ambiguation of philosophical meanings.

We can still observe, however, that Derrida (or Nishida) composes his nomothetic utterance in the form of an individual text. I take the Derridean (or Nishidan) "text" here to mean the entire corpus of his writings. It is ultimately these individual texts, with their characteristic signatures, that "make sense," or are sense-constituting, and thus become exemplary significations in the world-history of philosophy.

Now Derrida's text is sense-constituting in at least two recurrent ways. First, it proceeds to ambiguate the key semantic terms of a given philosophical text—that of Plato, or Rousseau, or Hegel, or Heidegger, for example. By so ambiguating these key terms it dissolves them into what Derrida calls the "inexhaustible adversity" of what funds them and into the "infinite absence" of what founds them.[23] That is what deconstruction is— an interminable analysis of the apparent surface of texts that simultaneously disseminates traces of interpretive supplements in a dynamically adversative form. Secondly, Derrida polarizes the history, or better, variety of texts in a new adversative set. For example, Derrida writes:

> All the metaphysical determinations of truth, and even the one beyond metaphysical onto-theology that Heidegger reminds us of, are more or less immediately inseparable from the instance of *logos*, or of a reason thought within the lineage of *logos*, in whatever sense it is understood: in the pre-Socratic or the philosophical sense, or in the anthropological sense, in the pre-Hegelian and the post-Hegelian sense. Within this *logos*, the original and essential link to the phone has never been broken.[24]

Derrida of course claims, nomothetically, to break the link, and therefore to be something else again. For "if reading and writing are one, as is easily thought these days, if reading is writing . . ."[25]

In brief, Derrida takes Heidegger's declaration of the closure of the metaphysical tradition from Plato to Nietzsche a step farther when he charges that the whole Western tradition, in one way or another, is "logocentric." He asserts that the Western philosophical tradition has always presupposed a concept of "identity" at the basis of its representational procedures, through which "Being" and its equivalents are presented (or re-presented) in ontological, epistemological, and semantic forms. Derrida's own project works precisely at "the subversive dislocation of identity in general, starting with that of theological regality."[26] To produce a form of non-edifying discourse has in fact been the common intent of a variety of so-called postmodern hermeneutical schools. But it is fair to say that these schools are iterating the same kind of allegation against "being" and "object logic" (representational logic) that has been issued in the texts of Nishida and the Kyoto School for the past sixty years. They are only now

catching up with Nishida's many-sided attack on onto-theologi-
cal discourse.

Like the Kyoto School, Derrida's agonistic method of discursive procedure reduces a richer, more complex multiplicity to an
adversatively polarized set. It is discursive in the literal sense of
running through—at least formally, or transcendentally—the entire multiplicity of philosophical texts to arrive at a characterization of their common "logocentric" form, which is then polarized against his own non-logocentric form. It compounds the
ensuing confusion by linking together the concepts of "Western"
and "logocentric." The tension between Western logocentricism
and putative non-Western non-logocentricism is then the generi-
cally significant form of Derrida's textual strategy. This is a
sense-making tension that overwhelms every possible alternative
discursive operation. It especially prevails over any intention to
discriminate among the principles and methods of the several
individual Western philosophers. Rather, Western philosophers
from the pre-Socratics to Heidegger—despite their self-conscious
endeavor to assert archic differences from one another—are all
lumped together under the rubric of "logocentric discourse."

It should be evident that Nishida's text, with its "logic of the
East" *(tōyōteki ronri)*, creates a similar fissure. Western texts are
characterized as all falling under the concept of "being" *(u)* while
Eastern texts are said to philosophize from the standpoint of
"nonbeing" *(mu)*. According to such an axiom, East is East and
West is West and never the philosophical twain can meet. Moreover, Nishida's "Eastern logic" with its "Oriental nothingness"
(tōyōteki mu) is the "concrete logic" while the several logics of
the West are "abstract." This same kind of semantic polarization
informs Nishida's reading of individual philosophical texts. Near-
ly all the major Western philosophers Nishida cites are said to
have "objectified" views of the self, or of the absolute, while his
own view articulates the truly "subjective" immediacy of experience in its nondual ground. Like Derrida, Nishida exemplifies his
own semantological form; but he does so at the expense of the
greater wealth and variety of sense-constituting principles and
methods that are to be found in the material history of philosophy. To the untutored reader, the many essential differences
among Asian philosophical texts are passed over as well.

Let us return to our analysis of Nishida's text. I have suggested that Nishida, in espousing a paradoxical method of articulation after 1927, *in principle* (that is, *in presupposition*) could not discriminate the essential variety of possible logical operators in the history of philosophical texts. For he discriminated according to a rule of disparity. It can even be seen that his method misses the mark in discriminating between the logics of Aristotle and Kant. To be sure, Kant's logic can be described as a "transcendental logic," in Nishida's phrase, in that Kant employs his method of analysis and synthesis in the service of delineating all the essential, a priori forms of pure reason (both theoretical and practical). But, at a generic level of characterization, this is precisely the synoptic, or problematic, method of Aristotle. The common procedure of Aristotle and Kant is to take up the various subject matters of philosophical discourse and to analyze them into their essential kinds according to a discriminative rule of genus and species, in pursuit of the architectonic (or "scientific") project of autonomous philosophical reflection (thought thinking itself). We have had occasion to observe that Kant, in his epistemological account in the first *Critique*, proceeds as a transcendental Aristotelian. In sum, the methodic procedure of Kant's critical philosophy, which refracts into the three *Critiques* for which he is famous, coincides with the synoptic, or problematic, procedural form of Aristotle's text. For if Aristotle's method is the differential analysis of subject matters according to the co-variable categorial determinations of the "four causes," the same kind of differential analysis of the parts or employments of pure reason subtends the discursive operation of Kant's several *Critiques*. Both philosophers proceed to exhibit the essential variety of forms in an architectonic fashion.

A full analysis, then, will reveal that not only do the texts of Aristotle and Kant coincide in method of articulation, but they are also affine in perspective (namely, the universal theoretical interest of the architectonic, or scientific, project) and in integrative principle (namely, pure reason, in its autonomy, completing its own internal project of self-reflection). It is thus possible to rethink Nishida's various characterizations of the allegedly different "logics" of Aristotle and Kant. But it then follows that many of Nishida's analyses will be subject to hermeneutical reinterpretation as well.

Taking the various threads of the discussion in hand, let us readdress from another perspective the issue of Nishida's text as a monumental importation and deconstruction of Western positions. As noted above, there would seem to be little argument against the peerless intercivilizational style of Nishida's philosophical discourse. But we have seen that the syncretic character of Nishida's text was first achieved, between 1911 and 1927, in a prevailingly dialectical (Fichtean) mode of articulation, and then, between 1927 and 1945, through a paradoxical form of expression. (It was in this second stage that the agonistic counterposition of the "logics" of Aristotle, Kant, and Hegel surfaces in Nishida's text.) Nishida's final logic of the religious consciousness becomes intelligible in the light of this paradigm shift in his own text.

Now these logical types can be discriminated adversatively, as in Nishida's text, or as part of a differential analysis in the synoptic mode of inquiry, one that discriminates an *essential variety* of types. The intention of the latter method is to produce a complete typology of the forms of discursive operation of texts. But what would a complete table of discursive modes consist of? Taking Nishida's own text as a point of departure, it would appear that he has correctly discriminated between the dialectical (sublational) and the paradoxical (agonistic) forms. By re-aligning the methodic procedures of Aristotle and Kant as a common type, we can observe a third kind. These now represent three distinct types of logic, or structural forms of categorial determination.

A fourth irreducible kind of logical operator can also be adduced from major texts in the history of philosophy. This would be the logistic, or computational, method of discursive operation. The logistic method is the form of textual articulation that intuits a variety of affine essences, ideas, or characters, and proceeds to relate them according to a rule of addition and subtraction. It is the method of adding clear and distinct ideas, as in Descartes, or of the association of simple ideas to form complex aggregates of ideas, as in Hume. Each idea, or unit of discourse, is a separate, independent integer; these integers can be added or subtracted in a mechanical, or aggregational, calculus. The *locus classicus* of this computational method is found in the text of Democritus, the discursive operation of which is subtended by a logic of atoms and the void. In modern times this method has become the logic of the computer—that is, of *+1* or *-1*; or alternately, of *1* and *0*. The *ars characteristica* subtending the articulation of Leibniz's numerous essays is perhaps the epigonic instance of the logistic form of categorial determination in systematic metaphysics.

Our differential analysis thus distinguishes four irreducible kinds of logical operators in texts: logistic, synoptic, dialectical, and paradoxical. Each is a generic type, admitting of numerous species and subspecies, in the global history of thought. But there is no logical or epistemic hierarchy among these types, since each can be legitimately employed as an infrastructural variable in a textual patterning of significance. Yet it is the synoptic method which legitimates the other types through its own taxonomic intention of discovering an essential variety of types.

From this vantage point we can look back upon the distance traversed by our analysis. To begin with, the claim to a "logic of the East" yields to a synoptic discovery of a generic type of paradoxical, or agonistic, articulation that is shared by a variety of texts in both the East and the West. Nishida and Kierkegaard, for example, employ the same kind of paradoxical logic. The discovery of this form leads to the subsequent discrimination of structural types, producing a set of four irreducible kinds of logical operators in texts, such that the contrast between "concrete" and "abstract" types is also seen as being true to a form. The appropriation of the term "concrete" thus appears as a favorite rhetorical device of both the dialectical method of argumentation, as in Hegel, and the paradoxical, as in Nishida.

In Nishida's 1944 essay "Toward a Philosophy of Religion By Way of the Concept of Preestablished Harmony," he sets out to reorder the metaphysical priorities of two major Western philosophers, Cusanus and Leibniz, from the standpoint of his own logic. But like every important philosopher, Nishida sets certain taxonomic presuppositions into play as soon as he begins to think out and write down his text.[27] The very dynamic of the constitution of meaning in philosophical texts entails this transformation of the general possibilities of discourse into a specific form of actualization as a significant text. But the major texts of Cusanus, Leibniz, and Nishida, each with roots in its own metaphysical and spiritual traditions, evidently constitute different meanings—they literally make sense in different ways. And they purport to do so at a foundational level of discourse. Philosophers are always exhibiting some degree of self-consciousness about their fundamental differences with one another. This essential pluralism of logical, or methodic, types will be seen to open up the whole subject matter of "the logic of the religious consciousness" to reconsideration as well. Since Nishida's text constitutes a pioneer effort in this direction in twentieth-century thought, we can turn to his various essays and find therein challenging materials for hermeneutical reflection on the possibility of inter-civilizational discourse itself.

We can conclude this postscript by focusing once again on the overall hermeneutic of Nishida's own powerfully assimilative text. Nishida's strategy of "transcending inwardly into the depths of noesis," with its obvious appropriation of the thought of Kant and Husserl, has been noted above. His incorporation of the thought of Aristotle, from the 1930s, is another striking example. It is clear, however, that Nishida "reads" these texts, as well as those of Spinoza, Leibniz, and other major Western thinkers, in his own way. Nishida's text is conspicuously marked by its own transcendental principle, its a priori of a priori—namely, that vanishing point of the self-actualization of the existential act that is simultaneously the self-actualization of the absolute. His key concepts of self-expression, self-reflection, and self-consciousness, and of the act as the self-determination of the concrete universal, and active intuition as the self-transformation of the place of absolute nothingness, are all returnable to this same nondual principle. It will also be seen that when Nishida cites traditional Zen and Pure Land texts, it is often to exemplify his own principle of the nondual but contradictory identity of the active religious self in its self-awakening character.[28]

Like any philosopher, Nishida sought for affinities to his own ideas in his own traditions. At the same time, he found many ideas of Western philosophers entirely congenial to his purposes. For over thirty years he rarely cited Eastern texts to illustrate his views. From the standpoint of comparative hermeneutics, it can be said that Nishida's text constitutes an important structural link in the networking of major philosophical texts of East and West. The irony is that this is true despite his own, and the Kyoto School's, agonistic claim to the contrary.

The positive genius of Nishida's philosophy, I will submit, consists in its articulation of his conception of an infinitely deep existential self grounded by a principle of absolutely contradictory identity. Only this infinitely deep self that is prior to our cognitive, aesthetic, and moral selves is the self that is religiously vivid and intense. And to Nishida it would appear that it is philosophy which most facilitates our awareness of this self:

> The philosophical standpoint is that of the self-reflection of the religious self in itself, not looking back on the intelligible world from the religious standpoint, and not making the content of the intelligible world its own content. It is not the standpoint where an absolute self constitutes the world, but that of self-reflection, or of the self-reflection of the absolute self.[29]

Nishida devoted his long philosophical career to saying this. He died saying this, even as the machines of war were raining bombs down on Tokyo just a short distance away.

But, of course, many philosophers have sought to philosophize from the philosophical standpoint. What we have is the variety of their intuitions, and the opportunity to reflect on their texts in our own.

Notes

1. *Nishida Kitarō zenshū* (The Collected Works of Nishida Kitarō), 2d ed. (Tokyo: Iwanami Shoten, 1965), 9:331–35. The collected edition is hereafter cited as *NKZ*.

2. *NKZ* 4:6.

3. See J. G. Fichte, *The Science of Knowledge*, ed. and trans. Peter Heath and John Lachs (Cambridge: Cambridge University Press, 1982). On Fichte's dialectical notion of the transcendental self's self-positing activity, see the editors' remarks, pp. xiii–xviii. See also Fichte's *The Vocation of Man*, ed. Roderick Chisholm (Indianapolis: Bobbs-Merrill, 1956).

4. *NKZ* 7; *Nishida Kitarō: Fundamental Problems of Philosophy*, trans. David A. Dilworth (Tokyo: Sophia University Press, 1970), especially vol. 2, subtitled "The Dialectical World."

5. On this point see Nishida's "The Problems of Japanese Culture," trans. Masao Abe, in *Sources of Japanese Tradition*, ed. Tsunoda, de Bary, and Keene (New York: Columbia University Press, 1958), 851–72.

6. In the essay that forms the final chapter of the second volume of *Fundamental Problems of Philosophy* (1934), "The Forms of Culture of

the Classical Periods of East and West Seen From a Metaphysical Perspective," Nishida proceeds from the premise that ". . . we can distinguish the West to have considered being *(u)* as the ground of reality, the East to have taken nothingness *(mu)* as its ground" (p. 237). It would appear that all the writings of the Kyoto School, and most writings on it, subscribe to this statement.

We should note, however, the independent influence of D. T. Suzuki on the Kyoto School. Suzuki's direct influence on Nishida's "The Religious Worldview" essay must also be taken into account. Suzuki wrote a series of works in Japanese on the subject of "Japanese spirituality" in the mid-1940s. The first of these appeared in 1944 under the title of *Nihon-teki reisei* (Japanese Spirituality). It was followed in 1946 by *Reisei-teki Nihon no kenketsu* (The Awakening of Spiritual Japan) and by *Nihon no reisei-ka* (Spiritualizing Japan) in 1947. Suzuki's 1944 work was in Nishida's hands when he wrote his "Religious Worldview" essay in 1945. Nishida's allusions in this essay to the spirituality of Shinran are especially indebted to Suzuki's work. And he cites Suzuki's authority in declaring that "at its root, Western culture has lacked [Shinran's] notion of [Amida's vow of] absolute compassion." The whole tenor of Suzuki's work is religiously and culturally chauvinistic, extolling Japanese Buddhist spirituality at the expense of other Japanese, Asian, and Western forms of religiosity. The subsequent writings of the post-war Kyoto School retain this agonistic strain of encounter theology. Its pre-war background can be traced to the thought of Nishida, Suzuki, Tanabe Hajime (1885–1960), and Watsuji Tetsurō (1889–1962), among others. In my judgment, all of these prominent Japanese philosophers confuse metaphysical and cultural predicates to some degree in their works.

7. Robert Wargo's *The Logic of Basho and the Concept of Nothingness in the Philosophy of Nishida Kitarō* remains the fullest articulation of the logical ramifications and entailments of the *basho* concept. Among other things, Wargo provides a semantic analysis and critique of the concept of "Oriental nothingness" in the writings of Shinichi Hisamatsu, an early exponent of Nishida's philosophy in the Kyoto School. Wargo's work is mainly focused on Nishida's *Ippansha no jikakuteki taikei* (1930), with its elaborate latticing of *basho* and their respective a priori.

8. A typical example of this paradigm of articulation in the Kyoto School writers appeared in a 1959 *Festschrift* for Paul Tillich, in which Takeuchi Yoshinori writes:

> Whenever the discussion arises concerning the problem of encounter between being and non-being, Western philosophers and theologians, with hardly an exception, will be found to align themselves

on the side of being. This is no wonder. The idea of "being" is the Archimedean point of Western thought. Not only philosophy and theology, but the whole tradition of Western civilization has turned around this pivot.

This is of course a reformulation of Nishida's own premise, as cited in n. 6 above. Takeuchi goes on to say:

All is different in Eastern thought and Buddhism. The central notion from which Oriental religious intuition and belief as well as philosophical thought have been developed is the idea of "nothingness." To avoid serious confusion, however, it must be noted that East and West understand non-being or nothingness in entirely different ways.

See Takeuchi, "Buddhism and Existentialism: The Dialogue between Oriental and Occidental Thought," in *Religion and Culture: Essays in Honor of Paul Tillich,* ed. W. Leibrecht (New York: Harper and Row, 1959), 291–365; the passage cited is on p. 292.

Hans Waldenfels begins his *Absolute Nothingness: Foundations of a Buddhist-Christian Dialogue* (New York: Paulist Press, 1980) by citing this pronouncement of Takeuchi. While the Kyoto School writers proceed to "encounter" the West in the agonistic mode of articulation, as represented by Takeuchi's "All is different in Eastern thought and Buddhism," Waldenfels, with his debt to Heideggerian and Rahnerian notions of "dialogue," proceeds to develop his own text in a dialectical mode.

For a more recent example of the agonistic literature of the Kyoto School, see Masao Abe, *Zen and Western Thought* (Honolulu: University of Hawaii Press, 1985).

9. See David A. Dilworth, "Nāgārjuna's *Catuṣkotikā* and Plato's *Parmenides:* Grammatological Mappings of a Common Textual Form," *Journal of Buddhist Philosophy* 2 (1984): 80–81, for a brief discussion of how Nāgārjuna's text succeeds in refuting all other possible views. It succeeds, that is, on its own terms; but this is true of every other philosophical text.

10. Robert Magliola, *Derrida on the Mend* (West Lafayette, Ind.: Purdue University Press, 1984), provides a masterful cross-cultural analysis of the semantic isomorphism between the logical operators of the texts of Jacques Derrida and Nāgārjuna, the Ch'an masters, and other Buddhist writers. I believe this structural analysis can be extended to Wittgenstein's *Philosophical Investigations,* which similarly employs an adversative logical operator in its central concept of *differing* language games in the existential forms of life.

11. *Parmenides* 166B, in *Plato: Collected Dialogues*, ed. Edith Hamilton and Huntington Cairns (New York: Pantheon, 1961), 956. See Dilworth, "Nāgārjuna's *Catuṣkotikā* and Plato's *Parmenides*," 91–98, for a fuller discussion of how Plato's *Parmenides* can be read as mapping the same grammatological space, and indeed as encompassing Nāgārjuna's four-cornered logic of negations *(catuṣkotikā)*.

12. F. H. Bradley, *Appearance and Reality* (Clarendon: Oxford University Press, 1893). This does not imply that Plato's and Bradley's texts are alike in all essential respects.

13. Hume ends his *Enquiry Concerning Human Understanding* with such a denunciation of Berkeley. He begins his *Enquiry Concerning the Principles of Morals* on the same note. See David Hume, *Enquiries Concerning Human Understanding and Concerning the Principles of Morals*, with Introduction and Analytical Index by L. A. Selby-Bigge, 3d ed. (Oxford: Clarendon Press, 1975), 149–75, and 169–70.

14. Murasaki Shikibu, *The Tale of Genji*, trans. Edward Seidensticker, 2 vols. (New York: Knopf, 1976), 2:1042.

15. *The Pillow Book of Sei Shōnagon*, trans. Ivan Morris (Baltimore: Penguin Classics, 1971), 181.

16. See Rosalie Colie, *Paradoxia Epidemica: The Renaissance Tradition of Paradox* (Hamden, Conn: Shoe String Press, 1976).

17. Shakespeare's "The Phoenix and the Turtle," stanzas 6–12, in *William Shakespeare: The Complete Works* (New York: Viking Press, 1979), 1439; as cited in Justus Buchler, *The Main of Light: On the Concept of Poetry* (New York: Oxford University Press, 1974), 70–71.

18. *The Collected Poems of Wallace Stevens* (New York: Knopf, 1964), 392.

19. See Walter Watson, *The Architectonics of Meaning: Foundations of the New Pluralism* (Albany, N.Y.: SUNY Press, 1985), 73ff.

20. *NKZ* 12:265–68.

21. Jacques Derrida, *Dissemination*, trans. Barbara Johnson (Chicago: University of Chicago Press, 1981), 64.

22. *Ibid.*, 98.

23. *Ibid.*, 70.

24. Jacques Derrida, *Of Grammatology*, trans. G. C. Spivak (Baltimore: Johns Hopkins University Press, 1976), 10–11; cited in Magliola, *Derrida on the Mend*, 3. Logocentric discourse's "essential link to the phone" refers to Derrida's contention that speech, the *phoné*, privileges meaning under the presupposition of ontic and epistemic presencing; he intends to displace the "phone" with "writing," which always entails a supplemental tracing of a presence in its absence.

25. Derrida, *Dissemination*, 63.

26. *Ibid.*, 86. An excellent summary of Derrida's critique is found in Magliola, *Derrida on the Mend*, 3–11 and *passim*.

27. It can be said that Nishida's text, with its paradoxical form of articulation, consistently and systematically makes two arbitrary choices. Both pertain to his (mis-)reading of Aristotle. First, Nishida always interprets the "logics" of Aristotle and Kant as distinguishable in kind; secondly, he tends to conflate Aristotle's logic with what I have called the logistic type. He considers the logic of modern Western science, for example, to be the "logic of objects" or "object logic," which he in turn equates with the Aristotelian logic of the grammatical subject. Here Nishida appears to have misapplied Husserl's concept of noematic determination.

28. Nishida's text exhibits a continuous play on the multiple nuance of *jikaku*—self-awareness and self-awakening—in a dynamic, world-realizing mode. But it would constitute another study to explore the hermeneutical possibilities of this point. In his interpretation of Zen and other Mahayana texts, does Nishida "read" those texts by way of his own principle of concrete immediacy and identity, as he tends to do in his reconstruction of the texts of Bergson, Kant, Fichte, Cusanus, Leibniz, and other philosophers? Or is his principle semantically isomorphic with the fundamental principle of those Mahayana Buddhist texts themselves? Or, yet again, is it only one of several principles that might be discerned in a comparative analysis of Mahayana Buddhist texts? Certain streams of Zen, for example, may appeal to Nishida precisely because he finds in them what he is looking for—namely, the existential stress on active self-reliance, self-acquirement, self-cultivation, self-practice, and the like. Nishida even finds this same element in Shinran's self-awareness that the compassionate vow of Amida is "for the sake of myself alone."

29. Kitarō Nishida, *Intelligibility and the Philosophy of Nothingness: Three Philosophical Essays*, trans. Robert Schinzinger (Honolulu: East-West Center Press, 1958), 139.

Index

⌷HAWAI⌷ Production Notes

This book was designed by Roger Eggers.
Composition and paging were done on the
Quadex Composing System and typesetting
on the Compugraphic 8400 by the design
and production staff of University of
Hawaii Press.

The text and display typeface is Trump.

Offset presswork and binding were done by
Vail-Ballou Press, Inc. Text paper is Glatfel-
ter offset Vellum, basis 50.